The Last Few Years

A Memoir of Life, Death and What Happened Next

Kathi Carey

Copyright © 2020 Carey-it-Off Publishing

All rights reserved.

ISBN: 978-1-7346991-0-4

Dedication

This book is dedicated to my Mom, Teddy Carey,
the woman who taught me what being
an independent woman really is
and to my husband, David,
who taught me what compassion
really means

Foreword • Acknowledgments

1	The Beginning	1
2	Thanksgiving	7
3	She Ain't Heavy, She's My Mother	15
4	The Fall	23
5	Don't Fence Me In	29
6	Like Mother, Like Daughter	41
7	Christmas	47
8	Easter	59
9	Mother's Day	67
10	The Last Day	75
11	The Funeral	81
12	The Aftermath	87
13	The Lawsuit	95
14	Repercussions	111
15	Epilogue	119
16	Final Thoughts	123

About the Author

KATHI CAREY

Foreword

It's been over five decades since Kathi and I first met, and over many lapses of time and space we seem to intersect at the oddest moments. Feeling cranky from several months of Covid-19 induced isolation, I chanced upon a picture of Kathi online for, I think, a sports channel ad. The effervescent image had been photo shopped as a blonde bombshell cheerleader, but there was no doubt about it: Kathi's image from years past, had been filched and what better time to make bank at CNN's expense than now? And while August is way too early for annual Christmas greetings, I emailed the image to a bemused woman who saw no reason to be litigious over a model she believed not to be herself. It IS her, I'm pretty sure, and I'm sorry that she doesn't see it. But after reading this book she has authored, I can see why she might not be interested in re-entering the hallowed halls of justice any time soon.

Hers is a story that I've sadly heard in other iterations; the account of her mother; a smart and pretty woman raising a family within the tight bonds of mutual affection, optimistic ambitions and religious devotion who, perhaps blessedly, passes on before she can witness the unraveling of everything she sacrificed to create. Kathi pens a tale that, in one way, we all wish we could tell; a story of meeting our mother as a friend, a confidant—a whole person.

KATHI CAREY

What would we give to know our mothers as real people? Kathi took the opportunity to do just that, and to paraphrase Dinah Craik, in this small volume she "takes the contents of her mother's heart, chaff and grain together, with gentle hands sifts it, keeps what is worth keeping, and with a breath of kindness, blows the rest away." Mrs. Carey, Teddy, I remember your laugh, I remember your delicious pot roast dinners, and your great big goodnight kisses at sleepovers. You are missed. I wish your family future healing.

—Lisa Jones
Friend, Mother, Writer

Acknowledgments

Those who know me well know that I'm a very private person—I'm not one to "wear my heart on my sleeve." So this book and the revelations therein may come as somewhat of a surprise since I spend much of it baring my soul and speaking about very private events and emotions. However, I'll admit that going through the death of one's mother after taking care of her for many years would qualify as a major life-changing event. As a writer, the only thing I could do to try and make sense of it all was to catalog my feelings in writing. So, I started a blog. Once the lawsuit started, however, it became obvious to me that I couldn't put all those goings-on in a public forum, especially while we were in the midst of going through them. So, what then? I couldn't imagine that all these musings would, in fact, become a book and even when I finished this I still wasn't convinced that anyone would actually want to *read* it.

So, I have to thank Kevin Courtright for giving this its first read-through and encouraging me to go ahead and publish it. He knew my mother before her death and he told me he found the book informative and interesting and he felt that others, even strangers, would too. I also have to thank Dave Balch, a dear friend who knows all about care-taking and someone with whom I have been able to talk about the difficulties inherent in that lonely task. Finally, I have to honor my husband, Dave. He did the yeoman's work of taking care of my mother, his mother-in-law, while holding down a business and living life. I frankly don't know how he did it. He truly is my hero.

KATHI CAREY

One

The Beginning

I didn't cry that day...nor for many days afterward. I often wondered why? Having spent most of my professional life in the entertainment business, first as an actress and now as a writer/director, I've seen and participated in scenes of death and dying where the living break down, sobbing over the lifeless form of the loved one left behind. But I was strangely bereft of emotion the day my mother died. There were so many things to be done. Perhaps that was it—my practical side kicked in as it had so often in the past. Did I get this from her?

When my father died *she* was the one who comforted everyone at his wake, and I imagined that later, alone, was when she finally broke down and let her emotions flow, although I wasn't there to witness it. It was how I reacted when my husband had his first, minor, heart attack and then his second, major one. He didn't die from either one, thank goodness, but the second was so serious that the surgeon who operated on him for over 2-1/2 hours told me, rather bluntly, that he should have. "This was the widow-maker," he said. "He's lucky to be alive." He spent the next 8 days in intensive care with a balloon pump beating for his heart. I became the model of efficiency those days and in the days that followed: calling family members, marshaling the elders of our Church to come and give him blessings, putting my own career on hold so that I could run his business from the hospital. It was only when I went home, alone, at night that I allowed myself to actually *feel* the emotions that tumbled and bubbled, just below the surface.

It all started 2-1/2 years earlier. Well, actually, it had *really* started about 17 years earlier. The 4th of July, 1999. My husband, David, and I were visiting my mom for the weekend. We often went to see her or had her come visit us after my Dad passed in June of 1992. Both of my brothers had moved across the country shortly after his passing so we were the only family she had in somewhat close proximity—and we were 400 miles away. We didn't like the idea of her being alone, so we made the trek from Southern California to the Bay Area as often as we could. On this day we had packed the car and were getting ready to return to L.A. when she fainted—just fell unconscious on the bed right in front of us. I had only seen my mother faint once before when I was a little girl and she had done the exact same thing: fainted on the bed. At that time the doctor said she was anemic and prescribed iron pills. This seemed different. By the time the paramedics arrived, she was awake, alert and, so typical of her, uncomfortable with everyone making such a fuss. Then it happened again—right in front of them and, thankfully, while she was hooked up to their heart monitors. Her heart rate dropped to 30.

This demanded an immediate trip, with lights and siren, to Stanford Hospital where the cardiologist ultimately decided she needed a pacemaker. We were told how lucky she was we were present when this 'event' happened: most people find out they need a pacemaker when their heart rate drops, they lose consciousness and then either (a) fall and break something (like a wrist, leg, ankle) or (b) get into a car accident. It usually takes the doctors a little sleuthing to find the underlying cause for the broken limb or the accident. The doctor advised us that she shouldn't really be living alone anymore—400 miles was a little far away, in his mind, for the closest relative as we couldn't come running in an emergency.

After some talk with my brothers, one of whom lived with his wife and 4 kids half in Virginia and half in Orlando, Florida and the other, who lived with his wife in a suburb of Kansas City, and a lot of talk with mom, it was decided that she would come live with us in Southern California. Ultimately, she was the one who made the decision—it was, after all, her life and she was going to do what *she* wanted to do. I believe that decision was made for several reasons: first she enjoyed her visits with us—she had been coming to visit regularly since my father had died in order to participate in a film/tv repertory company with which I worked. You see, she had always yearned to be an actress, ever since she was a girl.

The fact that I was making a living, both as an actress and as a writer/director *for* actors (as well as a consultant for them) made it easy for me to welcome her into the company and for her to start working, too. She was finally living her dream although at a long distance. So when the opportunity presented itself to move in together and start acting full time, well, I think that was icing on the proverbial cake.

Ahh… if we had only known the road we were about to walk down. As they say—hindsight is 20/20. And yet, I don't believe we would have made a different decision, even knowing what was to come.

That was, really, the beginning.

Two

Thanksgiving

Thanksgiving and Christmas were holidays I spent with my parents at their home in the Bay Area. Always. Even after I got married and had in-laws to consider. I used to ask my husband if he wanted to swap holidays—spend Thanksgiving with his family and Christmas with mine (because there was *no way* we weren't spending Christmas with my family...more on that later). But he liked spending time with my family and, since his mother was less accepting of me in the beginning of our marriage, we just gravitated towards the Bay Area for the holidays. After my Dad passed away, we continued the practice of driving up to the Bay Area to spend time with my Mom.

After we moved Mom down to L.A. we started spending

time with Dave's family. First it was at his mother's home in Santa Clarita and then, after she passed and that home was sold, the gatherings were often held at his brother's home in Huntington Beach or his sister's place in Woodland Hills. For some reason the gatherings were never held at our place in Sherman Oaks, even though it was certainly big enough to host a gathering. We were always told that it was because we had cats and many of the siblings were allergic. I was always a little suspect that, even though they liked me now, they weren't *quite* ready to spend lots of time at my house—it just wasn't as comfortable as hanging at one of theirs would be. I understood and it was fine.

My Mom was always game to go with us, wherever we wanted to go. She was almost a fixture—it became known that wherever Kathi and Dave went, Teddy went, too. That included family dinners, movies, fireworks, even weekends away. We enjoyed having her with us—she was fun to have around. I believe she enjoyed going places with us—heck, it was better than spending time alone at home. And she loved spending time with family.

The Thanksgiving before my Mom fell, which would have been in 2013, we spent at Dave's brother's home in Huntington Beach. The weather was cool, but nice, and the family was all in attendance. These gatherings were always a great time to catch up on what everybody was doing and have a nice visit. They weren't quite as interesting for my Mom, especially as she got a bit older, as she wasn't as mobile as she had been before. So she mostly sat in a chair while people flitted around her… here and there. I'm sure she felt a bit 'left out' at times as the conversation drifted from room to room, as dinner was cooked and served, and she was unable to go with it. This Thanksgiving we also became aware that, sometime after dinner, she wasn't feeling that well and we decided we would probably leave early. That didn't happen. After several trips to the restroom, my Mom got explosive diarrhea. Oh boy! Not only was it embarrassing for us, but I'm sure it was mortifying for her as well. We didn't have any of our usual supplies since this was a total surprise and we weren't expecting anything like this to happen. So, while I stayed with her in the bathroom, Dave went to a local drug store to buy some adult diapers, gloves, wipes, some garbage bags and a new pair of pants (for her). Once he came back and we got her (and the bathroom) cleaned up it was late and everybody else had gone home. We decided that from that point forward we were going to have to travel with her as if we had a baby—diapers, wipes, gloves and an extra pair of pants at the ready at all times. Since we have never actually *had* children this was all new to us. *This is what our lives had come to?* What fun!! We had no idea what was to come.

Dave and I never actually planned to *not* have children. I think he would've made an excellent father—he is such a warm, giving person, although he probably would've spoiled any child we had. However, after we had been dating for several years I started having seizures. Grand Mal seizures. We didn't discover what was going on right away. The first couple happened when I was at home, alone. I would wake up, face-down on the floor, time had passed and I was disoriented and exhausted. I remember coming out of the second seizure not knowing what day it was or where I was supposed to be—just feeling that I was supposed to be *somewhere*. I had the presence of mind to call Dave at work and ask him what day it was and if I was supposed to be somewhere and, of course, he told me I was supposed to be at work. Work??!! Heavens! Where did I work? At the time I was working at several different jobs. That particular day it was at a department store. I quickly called them and apologized for being late and told them I'd be there ASAP. However, when I arrived they sent me home *immediately*. I must've looked extremely unwell.

It wasn't until I had a seizure in front of Dave that we started to understand that something serious might be happening to me. We had been in Las Vegas, performing at the Sahara, and had driven home, arriving just in time for him to go to work (he worked the graveyard shift) and for me to go to sleep. He came over when he got off of work and as I was eating breakfast I had one of my Grand Mal seizures. Poor Dave. I think he freaked out completely. Since I have never seen myself in the midst of one of these I can only surmise that it must look scary. He called 9-1-1, then my Mom (who didn't answer) and then my Dad at his office. Once I came out of the seizure I was okay—the paramedics really couldn't do anything for me and, after a short trip to the doctor, I rested for the rest of the day. Dave went back to work, but after being there for only an hour or two he called from work and, over the phone, asked me to marry him.

Now, we had *talked* about getting married so this didn't feel like it was coming out of the blue, and the way he asked, it didn't feel like he was asking me *NOW*. So, of course I said, "Yes, we've talked about this…and you know that I want to get married in June so it will probably be next year." (This conversation took place in the middle of June). He said, "No, I mean tonight." Oh. Well, <u>that</u> was a shock. He explained that he didn't want me to go through this all alone, that he had great insurance (through his job) and I had none. It just didn't make sense for us *not* to be married. We could go back to Las Vegas and, since they do weddings 24 hours a day, get married right away. I said "yes", he left work and came right over. We flew to Vegas that night not expecting to stay any longer than it would take to actually have a quickie wedding ceremony: no luggage, no makeup, no toiletries. Basically we were dressed for a wedding—he in a white suit, me in a white dress.

Now, while it's true you *can* get married in Las Vegas 24 hours a day, what they don't tell you is that you have to have a marriage license and the Courthouse is only open until midnight. We arrived *after* midnight. Oops. Our friend and musical director/arranger, Pat Valentino, was working with Flip Wilson at the Sahara and he offered to let us crash in his room. However, since we hadn't brought a change of clothes or any toiletries, we couldn't really sleep. So, we sat there for awhile, then wandered the hotel and ultimately wound up at the gift shop, buying 'placeholder' rings for the ceremony later that morning. First thing in the morning the limousine came and picked us up, took us downtown to the Courthouse where we obtained our license, and whisked us back to the "We've Only Just Begun" wedding chapel, then went and picked up Pat to be our witness. We were married on June 19th so, technically, I got my June wedding.

Here was the fly in the ointment: my parents, and

especially my Dad, had always wanted to throw me a GREAT BIG WEDDING with all the trimmings—especially since I am their only daughter. My Mom had always dreamed of me wearing her wedding dress and had kept it, wrapped in blue paper, in her cedar chest just for that purpose. My Dad had always dreamed of giving me away with all their friends in attendance. What to do? Eep! Well, instead of telling them about our Vegas nuptials, we kept them secret—until now (don't ask me <u>how</u> I kept this secret all these years!). We went ahead and let my parents plan and give us the big wedding they always wanted on August 30, with 300 of their closest friends (and a few of mine) in attendance. That took place at Holbrook Palmer Park in Atherton, with a lovely string quartet playing the music. It was a beautiful ceremony all the way around. So now I have two special days to remember and celebrate.

What does all this have to do with kids? It turns out that it doesn't matter what medication you take to control seizures (meaning any or *all* of the different ones), they *all* cause birth defects. These range from mild to very serious. The chances of the baby with one or more of these potential birth defects are 20%. That's 100 times greater than the chances of having a Downs Syndrome baby for a woman over 35 (.02%). Going off the medication while pregnant is no better—having a seizure while pregnant causes different and worse birth defects. So, that was that – Dave and I decided we would not have kids.

Oh, but that's not entirely true. As we got older, and my biological clock started ticking *very loudly*, I yearned to have a child. With Dave. We investigated the possibility of having our own biological children via a surrogate and I talked to a doctor who had helped a friend of mine do just that. When he found out the reason I wanted to try that approach, he suggested that I try having my own kids first, since a 20% chance of birth defects meant an 80% chance of having a healthy baby. I listened to his advice, went off birth control and we tried. In fact, I never went back to birth control. It seemed like I might've gotten pregnant a couple of times and spontaneously miscarried. I'll never be sure. But what I *am* sure of is that I wasn't meant to have kids. It made me sad for a while but then my Mom moved in with us and it ended up that, as she became dependent upon us, taking care of her was very much <u>like</u> taking care of a child—one that was digressing towards being an infant. Only… an infant in an adult body which, truth be told, wasn't quite as easy.

Three

She Ain't Heavy, She's My Mother

In life we make lots of decisions—some are intellectual decisions, some are emotional decisions and some are a combination of both. I believe that the decision to move in together with my Mom and take care of her was more an emotional decision, ultimately. Yes, we weighed the pros and cons of having her live on her own. We also talked about what it would be like if she had to move into a nursing home. And we discussed the possibility with her of moving in with either one of my brothers instead of with us. Ultimately she decided to move in with us.

But as time wore on and her aging brought with it different challenges, I wondered if we were like the proverbial frog and the pot of boiling water: throw the frog into the boiling water and it will automatically and instinctively jump out to save it's own life. But put it into the pot of cool water and slowly bring that pot to a boil and it will boil to death. We were slowly taking on more and more duties and dealing with more challenges as time wore on.

When Mom first moved in with us she was quite independent and insisted, in fact, that we honor that: she wanted to drive her own car, travel, cook for herself in her own kitchen, basically "do her own thing" without us hovering about. We were fine with that arrangement, although we secretly enjoyed the fact that she was right down the hallway or downstairs "just in case anything happened that needed our attention." Within the first year she had a TIA (transient ischemic attack), which is a small stroke for the laymen. We didn't believe it was the first one. It had seemed that she had had some smaller, earlier ones before she moved to L.A. However, this one seemed bigger than all the rest. It left her with no permanent damage except aphasia, which is an inability to 'find your words' or remember words, phrases or names. This was most frustrating to my mother who was quite smart (she had attended Stanford University on a merit scholarship, after all). One of her favorite past-times had been doing daily crossword puzzles. She loved them. In fact, one Christmas after my Dad passed we got her a great, big crossword puzzle book. Unfortunately, she never finished it as she abandoned the crosswords after this TIA. She found that she could just no longer think of the words anymore. What it also meant was that my generally loquacious mother became, after a period of time, quiet. She just kind of stopped speaking. Now this was a woman who would start conversations with complete strangers in line... anywhere. So the fact that she almost ceased talking, except to the family, was extraordinary. It started slowly at first. She would start a sentence, come to a word that she just... couldn't... find in her brain and she would try and try and try and then give up in frustration. After that kept happening over and over she ultimately gave up in defeat. Aphasia.

A few years after that she was hospitalized with what was diagnosed as chronic pancreatitis. It seemed that she had adopted a diet that wasn't really healthy for her. So, this meant that we needed to cook all her meals for her. Now by this time we were fixing all of her dinners, but now it meant that we needed to fix her breakfast and lunch, too.

I don't want to make this sound all gloom and doom. During this time we also had a lot of fun. For her 80th birthday we bought a used motorhome from a friend and took my Mom on a 1-month cross-country tour to visit her family and friends that were scattered all over the country. She got to spend time with her grandchildren, her sisters, her childhood and college best friends, as well as my brothers and their families. We also spent time with Dave's sister in Texas and my best friend in Albuquerque, New Mexico. The motorhome broke down several times (it was old and used, did I mention that?) and we had many adventures along the way and I know she had a lot of fun on that trip.

My mom also was able to travel the East Coast with her sister and do a tour of National Parks with a friend from Singapore.

The biggest trip we took was a trip to China. This was an awesome trip that my Mom and I took together that lasted over 2 weeks. We visited all the major attractions, including the Forbidden City, the Terra Cotta Warriors, The Great Wall, Shanghai, and a nice boat trip up the Yangtze River before they finished the 3 Gorges Dam project.

We had planned a riverboat trip to Russia, which included visits to both Moscow and St. Petersburg, but she was in a car accident just a few days before we were to leave and she hurt her back very badly. Unfortunately we had to cancel that trip and were never able to reschedule it—she developed chronic back pain that never went away.

As time wore on we did everything with my Mom... or rather, she did everything and went everywhere with us. Some of these things were activities and events that were part of our lives and she accompanied us, like film festivals, and some of them were things that we scheduled specifically because we knew she would enjoy them, like the Hollywood Bowl. But whatever it was, we were like the 3 Musketeers – Dave, Kathi and Mom. She enjoyed it and we enjoyed having her with us. Which was why she became a regular fixture at the family dinners.

However, there were a few things that she just couldn't participate in. For instance, in the beginning of October 2012, I shot a movie. This was something I had written and was producing and directing and it was to be an 8-day shoot.

Normally we would leave Mom to her own devices while on these shoots—it wasn't that I wouldn't be around, but my days would be long (14-16 hours) and that meant I wouldn't be home much for the duration. Additionally, due to the fact that Dave generally handled the catering for the shoots, it meant he wouldn't be around, either. The last time we did one of these longer shoots (also 8 days) was in 2005 and we hadn't worried about leaving Mom home alone during that time. However, this was 7 years later. We had been cooking all of her meals due to her very restricted diet (chronic pancreatitis, remember?) and the upshot of that meant that if she ate too much fat in any one meal she couldn't digest it—it would sit in her stomach for a day or two, and then she'd throw it up. Not pleasant for her. Best to not leave her to her own devices, as she'd probably go back to eating the crappy food that got her there in the first place. So, I asked my brother if he would mind if she stayed with him for a couple of weeks while we shot the movie. He said that would be fine and we sent her off to stay with him and shot the movie. One less thing to worry about. Or so we thought.

Unfortunately, Mom came back with a UTI. In fact, the UTI had progressed to the point that by the end of the day, when I checked on her, I thought she had had a stroke. I called 9-1-1; the paramedics came and determined that she was in sepsis (which looks like a stroke in some cases). And off to the hospital she went. Yikes!

Thus the beginning of recurrent UTIs. It seemed like from that point forward she got one after the other until she died, actually. One of the side effects of UTIs can be brain fog or confusion, besides the need to urinate constantly. My mother, being a proud and refined woman, refused to wear a diaper for the longest time. Once she started to wear one (I actually think she didn't know she was wearing it because they're just like pull-up underpants) she refused to use it. But because she was now in her 80s, approaching her 90s in fact, and the threat of dying from a fall was very real, we didn't want her getting up in the middle of the night, in the dark, and walking to the bathroom. So Dave, bless his heart, started to sleep downstairs nearby. Ultimately, he set up a chair and then a bed in her room and slept in there with her so he could wake up and help her during the night. He did this for over 3 years until her death. What a saint. It wasn't that she was heavy, by any means, but by this point I, too, had ruptured a disc in my lower back (in the Fall of 2013) and was developing my own chronic back problems and just couldn't lift her, no matter how little she weighed.

Because she seemed confused from time to time we asked her doctor specifically if she was developing dementia. He said no. He indicated it might be as a result from the UTI and asked us to keep track of when she seemed particularly confused. Once we did that we concluded that he was right. Although, once she got C-Diff, things really began to change. But I think I'm getting ahead of myself here.

Four

The Fall

"Mister David, Mister David! The Grandma fell down!" Epi called. Epi was our handyman. He was fixing the bay window in the room near my mother's. It was late morning, January 6, 2014. My husband ran downstairs and I followed. As best as we could make out, my mother had been sitting on the edge of her bed, putting on her shoes, when she lost her balance and fell from that position to the floor, landing right on her hip and crying out in pain. She groaned as she was in quite a bit of pain. David wanted to take her to the hospital or Urgent Care but she adamantly refused, and just wanted him to put her back in bed, which he did, vowing to check on her in an hour or two. She promptly fell asleep and we both went back to work.

My mom had been living with us, at that point, for 14 years and, for the last two, trips to Urgent Care and the hospital were a relatively common occurrence. At age 91, we knew she could leave us at any time, although we had no idea that *this* would be the inciting incident that would eventually lead to her death.

After a few hours, when the pain was worse, we decided a trip to Urgent Care was definitely necessary and my husband and I gingerly bundled my Mom into the car and away we went. They confirmed she had a broken hip and sent us to the hospital, about a block away. That they didn't take her in an ambulance was curious to me, and I commented to Dave about it at the time. It seemed that they were really opening themselves up to a lot of liability by sending her there with *us*. They did call ahead so she was whisked away into the hospital without all the red tape and waiting that usually accompanied her admissions there, which was a very good thing as the pain was getting worse and worse and the admittance often took hours (sometimes as many as 8 or 10).

Surgery followed the next day and the surgeon couldn't have been nicer. His own mother, almost the same age as mine, had undergone the identical procedure (not a total hip replacement but a repair with pins and rods) just a few months earlier and had recovered completely. He assured us that my Mom would be just fine. Dave had been very, very gentle with her so her hip was not displaced and she didn't need a total replacement—just a repair. A few days in the hospital were to be followed by 4 weeks of rehab in a nursing home and 2 more weeks at home where she could *not* put weight on her leg. This is where life started to become complicated.

Dave and I had recently decided to bring his business to the house. It had been months of discussions and it finally made sense: it was the beginning of 2014 and he wasn't getting as much walk-in business anymore—most of his work was being accomplished on-line. He already had an office in our home and it just didn't seem prudent to spend an exorbitant amount of money for a brick and mortar office. But the timing…oh, the timing. How would he move his office, keep his business going all while taking care of Mom. You would think, "Well, she's tucked away there in the nursing home, being taken care of by others, so you don't need to worry." Hah! Hardly. What with the pain and the surgery and all the disruption to her life, my mother was understandably feeling uneasy and apprehensive, which made her concentration on short-term items less effective. So, it seemed as though she couldn't concentrate on what you and I would consider everyday ideas like figuring out a new remote control to call the nurse (every new place, like the hospital, the nursing home, etc. had a different-looking, new-to-her call system). It became incumbent upon me to impress upon the nurses and caretakers how tenuous her situation was, especially now that she couldn't put *any* weight on that leg/hip. This meant that if she woke up in the middle of the night, she would take it upon herself to get out of bed and just go to the nearest bathroom by herself. Um, no. That would not be good. What actually ended up happening was that we needed to set up overnight stays to make sure she was watched like a hawk, wherever she was (other than the house). So, the nursing home wouldn't be any different. We needed to set up a system whereby someone would stay with her each night she was there so that she wouldn't just climb out of bed in the middle of the night when she felt "the urge" and re-break that hip by putting all her weight on it. For the first week it was, you guessed it, Dave. I offered, but he wouldn't hear of it. Due to the ruptured disc in my lower back from 3 months earlier, I was wearing a back brace so sleeping in a hard metal chair would probably have put me back in bed, flat on my back, in excruciating pain. Finally, after a couple of weeks, my sister-in-law came and spelled Dave so he could actually work and not be a zombie.

Oh, and did I mention? The day she was moved to the nursing home was my birthday. Normally, in the past, Dave, my Mom and I would have gone out to dinner to celebrate. This year? We helped move Mom into the nursing home. Needless to say, I was feeling sorry for myself and, between us, Dave and I called it "Crappy Birthday." When his birthday came a couple of weeks later, it was the day we had to take her for her check up with the surgeon – yay! Oh, the red tape just to have her leave the nursing home to go to a doctor's appointment! We could hardly believe it, especially given the fact that *they* weren't offering to take her. Dave had a "crappy birthday" too.

Many weeks later Dave's sisters decided to have a special birthday dinner for us (and his brother, who's birthday is a week before mine). This was planned weeks in advance but, as luck would have it, Mom ended up in the hospital for the weeks leading up to that day and they decided to release her...when? ON THAT DAY – a Sunday. Really?? Why they released her on a Sunday I'll never know. But the beautifully-planned Birthday dinner didn't happen as intended because we needed to spend hours on her discharge at the hospital. Oh, and come to find out they discharged her before they should have and she ended up back in the hospital. What a comedy of errors. Ahh…it made me realize that it's really JUST A DAY. Once she died it sort of brought it all into perspective—I should be celebrating every day because I'm alive and healthy.

Five

Don't Fence Me In

My Mom was always a very independent woman, even for someone who grew up in the 1920s and 30s during the Great Depression. Her theme song was "Don't Fence Me In" and she used to sit at the piano in my childhood home and play it. She had a very distinctive style when she played the piano: the melody was always played in the right hand in octaves, the left played the accompaniment in a rolling style, and at the end of each phrase there were little filigree flourishes that would cascade down from the highest part of the keyboard. She played every song this way. I'm not sure where she learned to play like this and she never taught me this style, even though she was my first teacher. "Don't Fence Me In" was the only song she continued to play after she moved in with us in Southern California. I'm not sure if she forgot the others or she just liked that one the best. I am sure it was that independence and strong spirit that made us think she would bounce back from the broken hip and surgery. Dave and I were so *sure* she would recover, be able to walk again and become semi-independent, like she had been before it all happened that when we decided to hire some help for her it was only on a temporary basis. Unfortunately, we were wrong.

As I mentioned earlier, my Mom's health had gradually declined during the time she lived with us. It was gradual, though, and happened over a period of years so it wasn't particularly noticeable until the last couple of years. And then things started to stand out in stark relief. One of those was her independence turning to dependence. It was an interesting but troubling development. My mother was literally changing before my eyes.

She had initially balked at the idea of living with her children. It was not what *her* mother had done—she had gone first to an apartment and then to a nursing home, which was where she lived when she finally passed. On the other hand, my dad's mother had opted to live with her children when she gave up her apartment. She had 6 children so it worked out that she would stay two months with each one, rotating around the country. I always liked it when my grandmother came to stay, but I believe it was difficult for my mother as the daughter-in-law. She felt she could never please her mother-in-law. I think it was these remembrances that colored her preferences as she got older and made her decide she would *never* live with her children. But then one day she was faced with the actual choice: either (a) move into an assisted-living facility or (b) live with one of her children. How does someone face a choice that they don't *really* think will ever come? I don't want to think about it for myself. I can imagine she didn't, either. So, when faced with that decision, she opted to come and live with us. Initially she wanted to make it clear that she would remain independent: driving her own car, preparing her own meals in her own kitchen, doing her own 'thing,' so to speak. We let her have her independence—drive her car, fix her meals and such—for as long as she was able, but were glad that she lived under the same roof so we could keep an eye on her. Ultimately, though, she really liked living with us and we liked having her here.

Interestingly enough, almost as soon as she moved in, she stopped cooking dinner. Before moving in together she made such a fuss, stating that "a woman has to have her own kitchen" that we found a home that had two kitchens. The main one (downstairs) and a second, smaller one in a 'bonus' room upstairs. We assured her that we would use the smaller, upstairs kitchen and the big one, downstairs, would be her domain. Truth be told, she would always cook for us when we came to visit and I liked my mother's cooking. However, after we all settled in she let my husband (who is the cook in our family) do all the cooking for her. She fixed her own breakfast and lunch for a while and then, after being diagnosed with chronic pancreatitis, we started to fix those meals, as well. I think she was just asserting her independence and, once she was there, she liked the idea of having someone do the domestic work that she had spent most of her life doing. I found it amusing and delighted in letting her think that she was as independent as she wanted to be, while still becoming more and more a part of our lives.

After she had the TIA that first year and went through the frustration of trying to communicate and then, ultimately, started to get quiet, I believe her independence started to shift to dependence. It was almost imperceptible at the time. It happened so gradually and over such a long period of time that it was difficult, if not impossible, to see that this was what was happening at the time. This was a profound change for someone who had been quite independent their entire life—she traveled alone, she went out to eat alone, she went to movies alone, she did volunteer work alone. This was a woman who raised her children in the '60s and '70s. Jacquie Kennedy was her role model. She had very few role models for independent women and she never had a career as such. Yes, she put my Dad through school, but once she started having children she became a stay-at-home mother. However, she actively volunteered and served on several boards of directors of cultural organizations throughout the SF Bay Area. So she really straddled both generations – the stay-at-home mothers and the original career women. It's interesting that all of her sisters had careers and continued working as they raised their children. And my father's only sister had a career, too, as she raised her children. I can only think that my Mother got her independence from her own mother, who had her own career as a top chef in a top hotel dining establishment in Oslo, Norway before emigrating to the United States.

Looking back I can see that I was resisting the fact that my mother was changing. I didn't want to accept it. In fact, I didn't want to *think* that she was changing. It was as if she was becoming the child and I was becoming the mother—I was losing my mother before she was even gone and it didn't feel fair. Eventually, though, even I could see that she was becoming more dependent—she needed me and I was glad we were there to tend to her.

The most telling thing, though, in her progression from independence to dependence, was that she didn't want to be left alone. My mother had always been very self-sufficient and quite happy to be alone for long stretches of time: like I said she liked solitary activities like reading and doing the crossword puzzles, and she didn't mind eating out, going to movies or traveling alone. This was all part of her independence and I think it's where I got mine. However, as she changed we found that more and more she wanted us around—she wanted us to watch TV with her, she wanted us to just "be" with her…she didn't want to be alone.

When they released my Mom from rehab and we brought her home she was one or two weeks from being able to put weight on her leg. So, since Dave was now working at home, he hired his former assistant to sit with her and call him whenever she needed assistance, as her bedroom was downstairs and Dave's office was upstairs and he didn't want to miss hearing her call. My office was on the other side of the rather large home and Dave still didn't want me to try to do too much, especially since Mom couldn't put any weight on her leg yet. But at the end of the first month when I looked at the bottom line, our income was down 50%. It was March. March is usually a good month for us. Our business generally doesn't slow down until the summer. This was bad. This meant caring for my mom during the day was taking Dave away from his clients to the point that we were losing money and soon wouldn't be able to afford to eat, much less stay in our home. Something had to be done. Maybe we could hire a nurse, just during the day, to care for my Mom until she got back on her feet again? This prompted a consultation with my brothers. Mom had a money market account and there was a bit of money in it. "Use it," they said. So we called around and got a recommendation for a Certified Nursing Assistant (CNA). We told her it would probably only be for a few months and she agreed. Aura was her name. She was very good with my Mom—conscientious and kind. However, after a few months my Mom wasn't getting any stronger. In fact, it appeared that the dreaded UTI had returned. The nursing home had sent her home with antibiotics and we were administering them, but they weren't doing any good. So back to Urgent Care we went. More antibiotics were prescribed. They didn't do any good, either. She finally wound up back in the hospital. She didn't have a UTI – she had C-Diff, which we found out she had contracted at the nursing home. The antibiotics had apparently only been keeping it at bay.

I had never heard of C-Diff before. Boy was I in for an education. Apparently C-Diff is one of the most virulent infections one can acquire…and it's often contracted in nursing homes, skilled nursing facilities and hospitals. It is a bacterial infection of the colon and can be fatal as it doesn't always respond to antibiotics. While Mom was in the hospital we had to put on gloves and gowns to visit her and she was very, very ill. But even then they sent her home after only about a week of being treated. She was still on an antibiotic, which we discovered was *not* effective. In very short order it was determined that she still had C-Diff and she had to be re-admitted to the hospital. Now I was *mad!* This wasn't just bad for her—this was a potential health hazard for us.

When the hospital decided, after another relatively short stay, that they were going to send her home again, I put my foot down. I went to the head of the hospital and told him, in no uncertain terms, that they would *not* send my mother home until (1) we would not be required to wear gloves and gowns to visit her and (2) he felt it was safe, and not a liability for the hospital, for her to use the public restroom downstairs on the first floor, right alongside all the visitors. They kept her for another week. I'm not sure what possessed me to become so fierce when dealing with these health care professionals, but when it came to my mom and her care, I was determined to make sure that they really took care of her. If you ever met me you would not call me outspoken. I'm not a shrinking violet either but I am often considered reserved and unassuming, so this was unusual for me. I think I was becoming like a mother to my mother – I needed to protect her and rise to the occasion.

As part of the C-Diff, or maybe as a result of it, my Mom developed 'forgetfulness.' It started benignly enough: a question here and there that was repeated. We would be driving her somewhere and she would ask, "Which direction are we headed?" Dave would answer and then, not a minute later, she'd ask the same question. Sometimes, when she'd ask the direction question several times in a row, Dave would answer, "Well, which direction do you *think* we're going, Mom?" She'd sit and think about it for a minute. Sometimes she'd answer and get it right—almost as if she'd heard and remembered Dave's previous answers. Sometimes she'd respond with, "I don't know." Again we asked the Doctor about it. Again he assured us it wasn't Alzheimer's—just the common after-effects of the C-Diff (it was quite a virulent infection, after all). For me, and for her, there was nothing 'common' about it. Oftentimes she *knew* she had forgotten something really important and it would frustrate her so badly that she'd chastise herself, calling herself 'dumb' or 'stupid.' We'd have to remind her that she was always very smart—she had a scholarship to Stanford, after all—she just had too many memories and they'd filled up her allotted space and some were 'falling out.'

In the last 12 months of her life her forgetfulness got much more pronounced. She got sundowners syndrome and it kicked in most every day. She'd panic because she couldn't even remember who *she* was, let alone anything about where she was, who we were or what was going on. Either Dave or I (or both of us) would reassure her that all her memories were intact, somewhere in there, and that she had something called 'sundowners'—that it happened when the sun went down and it wasn't unique to her. It seemed to soothe her that she wasn't alone in this and that her memories would return in the morning. Often, we would recount her life story to her, starting way back when she was in grade school. It was handy that she had written her life story some years earlier and, in starting to go through her things, we found it. Eureka! It stopped shortly after we all moved in together, but it was a treasure trove of information and, reading it, I definitely got to know my mother much better.

In recounting her story, Dave would sometimes say something deliberately wrong so that she would correct him and then he could say, "See, you really *do* remember!" That would reassure her, as well. Sometimes I would cry big crocodile tears and then laugh and tell her that she had erased my entire life. Then I would start to tell her all about when I was born, where I grew up and all the things I did. This usually jogged her memory and she'd reassure me that she did, indeed, remember me.

Unfortunately, it took three months, two different antibiotics (one of which cost us $1500 for the copay) and a loss of 45 pounds to conquer the C-Diff. At the end of the whole ordeal she was now down to 100 pounds. This was a woman who, just six months earlier, had weighed in at 150. It wasn't long after that, that Aura let us know she had accepted another job that paid her more than we could afford to match. I couldn't blame her – when we hired her we were still hoping that my Mom would return to the mostly-independent woman she had been before she fell. When 'they' say hindsight is 20-20 this is what they mean. As we were going through all this it was hope that got us through all the bad stuff—we had buckets of hope. Add to that the fact that my mother was very strong (she survived C-Diff, after all) and our minds were made up that she could recover and regain her strength. Little did we know that she was headed towards the end of her life. I'm not even sure she knew it at that point. But as I look back now I can see it so clearly.

I'm sure this is what my mother went through when she was caring for my Dad. His last year of life was not easy. He was on dialysis because of complications from Type II Diabetes. He had already lost a toe, gotten Diabetic neuropathy and lost the use of his legs and for the last few months of his life she, too, hired someone to help her take care of him. That last year I visited often, driving the 400 miles from Southern California to Northern California almost every weekend. One of the last times I came up I didn't drive as I came alone (Dave needed to stay back) – I flew up. I think Dad was surprised to see me as I had just left a few days' earlier but everyone just had a feeling that he wasn't going to last much longer and I didn't want to miss an opportunity to see him one last time. I took my Mom out to lunch on that visit and I could see that the whole ordeal was really wearing her out. She was just so, so exhausted from everything. I assured her that it wouldn't be much longer and she didn't believe me. I'm not sure if she just couldn't face losing him, if she was simply overwhelmed with it all or if she was clinging to the idea that this was going to go on and on indefinitely. But I could see it so clearly—the end was definitely upon them. He passed away just 3 days later. I think sometimes when we're in the midst of things it's so difficult to step outside ourselves and the situation and see what's *really* going on.

Aura was able to recommend someone else: Maria. So, we decided to try Maria. What a blessing. Maria came into our home and loved my mother like she was her own. She had the patience of Job and if anyone could nurse my Mom back to health, we knew it would be Maria.

Six

Like Mother, Like Daughter

I spent much of my life feeling that I was very different from my Mom. In fact, I always felt that I was much more like my Dad. I'm not sure what gave me this idea, but I was sure of it. Both of my parents were extremely smart. Check. Neither of my parents were particularly musically talented, and I am, so…? No way to know where that came from. Actually neither of my parents were particularly *artistically* talented and everything I *do* is somehow related to the arts: I started in music, made a living as a singer for a while, made a living as a dancer for a while (both ballet and jazz), pursued acting, am now a writer/director and my hobby is painting. And yet, the longer my Mom lived with me the more I realized that I am, really, more like her than I ever realized; which I found to be comforting and cool—somehow some of her rubbed off on me, after all, subliminally or otherwise, as I grew up.

Mom grew up feeling that she was not pretty. I don't know why because I look at photos of her as a young woman and she was very attractive. She certainly had lots of beaus. She even entered a local beauty contest when she was 19 or 20 and won, although she chalked it up to the fact that she didn't really expect to win so she didn't care too much and just had fun. She wanted to make sure that any daughter of hers always felt beautiful, so she showered compliments on me my whole life, but I also grew up feeling unattractive…sort of an ugly duckling. I look back at pictures of myself and wonder why but, hey, I can't change what I felt at the time. I, too, entered a small beauty contest in my 20s and won and I chalked it up to the fact that I didn't really expect to win. Like mother, like daughter?

In her late teens or early twenties my mother fell in love, hard, for the first time. It was with a serviceman named Stan and they got engaged. World War II was well underway which resulted in a long-distance romance and, unfortunately, Stan was killed in the war by 'friendly fire'. I'm not sure my mother *ever* got over that. It was one of the reasons she said "no" 6 times when my Dad asked her to marry him. Yep! It took him 7 times to get her to say "yes" and she did so with the understanding that she still carried a torch for someone else. Can you even imagine? What love my father must've had for my mother! My Dad and I once had a conversation about that and, in a rare bonding moment, he opened up to me and told me that he knew he could win her over just by living with her, creating a life together, supporting each other, having children and growing old together. He was very wise, that man.

Come to find out he was also very romantic—he started writing her love letters right after they 're-met.' I never knew this about him until my mother passed and I found all of my father's letters in her things.

Their 're-meet' is a story in and of itself: My parents had gone to the same high school and even taken a debate class together, but had never really hung out in the same social circles—my mother used to say that my dad was much more popular than she. When they re-met it was right after the war; my mother was on a religious mission. I think she hoped that it would help her get over her broken heart. She was serving in Northern California, even though she grew up in Salt Lake City. My father's family just happened to move from Salt Lake City to Northern California during the war. My Dad was newly-returned from the war and he decided to go to a Church dinner/bazaar with his mother. My mother happened to be there. It was almost like fate stepped in. In fact, as kids, when they would tell this story, we used to tease them that they locked eyes across a crowded room and the rest was history. They would both laugh and say, "Not exactly." But, as it turns out, it was probably pretty close. Apparently, seeing my Dad at the event made enough of an impression on my Mom that she wrote about it in her diary (which we found after her death). Seeing my Mom at the event made enough of an impression on my Grandmother that *she* wrote about it in *her* diary (which we *also* found after my mother's death). A few weeks later, when my Mom was transferred out of that city, my Dad started writing her love letters. The love letters didn't stop until just before he passed. How's that for romantic? My Mom had plenty of choices when she returned from her mission—she dated lots and lots of guys, including a few dates with my uncle Dick (before she knew that her sister Lenore had a crush on him) and a bunch of dates with a friend of my Dad's named Gary. But I'd say that she chose the right guy, although I'm prejudiced.

Interestingly enough in sort of a parallel, I had a serious romance my first year in college with my piano professor. I was a piano major and I had done enough recitals and concerts and studied enough theory that I was able to completely test out of my freshman year of all of the required music courses (and buy the credits, too) so that at the end of my first year in college it was as if I had finished my sophomore year and I was now going into my junior year. My piano professor had attended the same university (as an undergraduate) I was attending and had gone onto graduate school elsewhere, returning to his alma mater to teach. His name was Terry; he was single, good-looking, about 6 years older than I and, in my mind, a catch. I fell…and hard. By the end of the first year we were serious and, as he returned to a school back east to work on his Doctorate, we got engaged. Alas, over that summer he broke up with me. But then curiously he quit his Doctoral program and moved to the Bay Area to be near me and the next couple of years would be an on-again, off-again rollercoaster romance between us that, finally, two-and-a-half years later ended once and for all. Even though we both lived on the Peninsula and, for a while, worked at the same company (I took a couple of years off school to work and go to night school) it just never worked out for us. Unlike my mother, I did *not* carry a torch for him for the rest of my life, and was able to meet a wonderful guy after I moved to Los Angeles. We've been married for over 30 years now. But, shockingly, her life was not so very different from mine and I found, as an adult, that my mother really could understand many of the things that I went through and be a good friend to me.

The hardest part of her decline during the last 5-6 years of life with her was losing that friendship—losing my best friend and my mother all at the same time. I could feel the change but I kept trying to hold onto the relationship we had, and then I'd get sad that she just wasn't there in the same way as she had been before. I was resisting the change and grieving the loss of our relationship. I had to find a different way to be with her because, after all, she was still my mother. This was all new territory for me.

Seven

Christmas

Christmas 2015. I had a premonition that this would be mom's last Christmas and so we set about making it the best one ever. Christmas had always been my mom's favorite time of year. She loved everything about Christmas: the music, the lights, the presents, the tree, the family all gathered together…everything. For as long as I can remember, there was always a big production in our home for Christmas—my father would go and find a tree (often with one or both of my brothers) and up it would go in the living room in front of the fireplace, next to the grand piano. Then my mom would go out into the garage and bring in the boxes which held the decorations and, usually, the Sunday evening after Thanksgiving we would all take part in decorating it. My dad would start by putting on the lights. Then my mom would take over, putting on the tinsel garland. We children were the *final* step and only after the lights and garland were complete would we be allowed to start placing the ornaments on the tree. Many of the ornaments were hand made by my mother, which is interesting because I, too, have hand made and/or hand-painted many of the ornaments for our tree.

The final piece de resistance would be the icicles, which had to be hand-placed one-by-one. As children, we were often tempted to throw handfuls of them on the tree (and, to be honest, there were many times I did just that), but my mother wouldn't hear of it. She wanted everything to be perfect and when we *did* throw those handfuls, she came in after we finished and re-did our handiwork, separating the clumps into neat rows. Then the lights would be turned on and they would stay on for the season, along with the constant sound of Christmas music. We had an advent calendar (the same one every year) and behind each date was a section of the poem "The Night Before Christmas." As the days marched ever closer to the Big Day, cards would collect on the two bi-fold doors of the living room, the presents would collect under the tree and our excitement, as children, would grow. Secretly, I think my mom's excitement grew as well—occasionally I would find her shaking a present or two when she thought no one was looking. It was almost like she became a kid again at Christmas.

So, in 2015 Dave and I put up the tree the day after Thanksgiving—we wanted her to have a nice long time with it.

THE LAST FEW YEARS

In the home we shared with my Mom, we always put the tree in the front room where she sat every day to watch her TV shows. By putting it up early this year she had 6 weeks of daily joy looking at the beautiful tree. One of us would turn the lights on every day so she'd get the full effect for the afternoon and evening. The next step was to fill the space under the tree with presents, although we couldn't really buy her a lot of stuff, since she didn't really *need* anything and whatever we bought her would probably be given away shortly. We didn't care—we were going to make sure that she had plenty: a nice warm blanket, some warm socks, a teddy bear (we always gave her a teddy bear since her name was Teddy), some peanut brittle from See's. Unfortunately, we couldn't give her any books to read anymore—her eyesight just wasn't good enough. And, of course, the Christmas music played whenever the TV wasn't on. One of my brothers was able to come stay a few days before Christmas, although he had to leave Christmas Day. My other brother was able to come out on Christmas Day so they overlapped a few hours and for those few hours she had all her children with her, which I'm sure made her very happy.

However, this year presented something new: an anxiety about Christmas I'd never before seen. For almost the entire month of December she kept grabbing either me or Dave in a panic, thinking that Christmas was over and she had somehow missed it OR she had forgotten to buy people presents. She'd be very upset, almost to the point of tears. We would reassure her that no, there was still plenty of time to buy presents and that Christmas was still 2 or 3 weeks away. It was a strange phenomenon. Maybe she sensed it was her last Christmas and she just didn't want to miss it—she wanted to be able to savor and remember it for the weeks that would follow.

The year my father passed, 1992, both my brothers moved away. One moved to Kansas City and the other moved to Virginia with his family, so by the time Christmas rolled around (my Dad passed in June) my mother was alone. Dave and I sensed it would be difficult for her. Really, really difficult. So, we spent extra time that year at her home, trying to make it a good holiday. We took her up to the City (she always called San Francisco "The City") to see the San Francisco Ballet Company perform the Nutcracker (a dance I had performed many years before) and we tried to convince her to come on one of our shopping sprees to the City, but she declined. We did, however, shower her with presents as it had always been my Dad's tradition to go a little overboard and buy my Mom more presents than their agreed-upon budget.

My parents always set a 'Christmas budget' that they would spend on each other. When I became a teen and then an adult my Dad often enlisted me in his plan to buy her things that would, often, exceed that budget, as well as help him wrap them to put under the tree. One year it was an expensive audio component set and one year it was jewelry. I remember he bought a mink stole one year (although that was without my assistance). Now <u>that</u> was a big present! It even had her initials embroidered inside. Back in the '60s, when he presented her with that gift, I'm sure it was a major status symbol and a big deal. Today, of course, I look at that mink stole and wonder what I should do with it, as it's not something I would ever wear. Yes, Christmas was her favorite time of year. I think it was the one time of year that she could forget, for a little while, the gnawing anxiety over money that the Great Depression permanently implanted within her and allow herself to feel special, have fun and enjoy life and her family.

One of the things that was always a tradition at Christmastime, since I was a child, was Christmas cookies. My grandmother (my mother's mother), Gunda, had been a chef at a prestigious restaurant in a large hotel in Oslo before she immigrated to the United States as a young woman. She came to the States in the early 20th Century, when women in the U.S. weren't allowed to work in such capacities, which meant she had to find work as a domestic once here. But she brought with her the tradition of making cookies for Christmas. Traditional Norwegian Christmas cookies, along with others she learned once here. When I was young we would receive a big box in the mail from her in early December filled with cookies she had made. There were so many in the box that we had enough to take plates to our teachers at school. My particular favorites were the Norwegian cookies: the Fattigman cookies and the Crinklies. I never knew the Norwegian name for the crinklies, just that they tasted yummy. When I was a young teen my grandmother came to visit us for Christmas one year and she taught my mother how to make those cookies. The crinklies were the easiest to make. They were similar to butter cookies, were formed in tins and baked in the oven. The Fattigman's (Poorman's) cookies were much more difficult—they took two days to make, were rolled thin, deep fried and had to be handled very, very carefully with the dough left quite sticky or it would become dry and the resulting cookies were not good. I can't even imagine how much time it would take my grandmother to make all these cookies to send to us and her other grandchildren—she had 5 children, who all had children, and I'm sure they all got a big box! After I got married I decided it was time for me to learn how to make the cookies, too. As I said before, the crinklies were easy. The Fattigman's were not. Dave, who is the cook in our family, helped me. Our first batch of Fattigman's were dry and unappetizing. But after that we got pretty good at making them. The crinklies were my Dad's favorite and I made a bunch for him for what would be his last Christmas. (Note: I can google the Fattigman and find a recipe that's not too very different from mine, but I cannot find anything resembling the crinklies or any Norwegian cookies made in tins. Hmm. Oh, and the Google recipe has you sprinkle the Fattigman with powdered sugar. Um, no. My grandmother would severely frown on that.)

By 2015, we had not been making the Fattigman's or the crinklies for several years. First, the crinklies were very rich (being mostly butter) and I didn't need the extra calories. Second, the Fattigman's consisted of mostly egg yolks and after Dave had had two heart attacks he was watching his cholesterol intake and the yolks of eggs have very high cholesterol. So, no Fattigman's for him. But the Fattigman's were my Mom's favorite (mine, too) so we had to make a small batch of them that Christmas just for her (and eat a few ourselves, too). We gave a lot of them away to our nieces who came to visit, but Mom was able to eat as many as she wanted. I haven't had the heart to make them since then as she was always there to test the dough and help me get it 'just right' so that the resulting cookies wouldn't be dry. Then again, I'm the only living descendant of my grandmother who still makes these cookies at Christmastime, as far as I know. If I stop, there's no one left to carry on this tradition and that makes me sad, so maybe I'll make them again every so often.

Many years ago I ran across an older Norwegian woman at church. I knew she was from Norway as she sounded much like my grandmother when she spoke—it's a very distinctive accent. That year at Christmas I took her a plate of cookies, which included both the crinklies and the Fattigman's. She recognized the crinklies right away as being from her homeland but she didn't recognize the Fattigman's, which was curious to me. I know the translation of Fattigman's is Poorman's. My grandmother told me that meant they were cookies that were made with ingredients that could be found on a farm: eggs, flour, a tiny bit of vanilla and a tiny bit of sugar (since poor people couldn't get much sugar or vanilla). Maybe that woman had been wealthy and had never had "Poorman's" cookies. Or maybe my grandmother was a purist as the pictures on Google show them being cut with a pastry cutter to make the edges rimply and then folded into knots before deep frying. My grandmother didn't make them that way – she just cut them with a regular knife and deep fried them "as is" and they came out in whatever funny shape they happened to be.

I had a feeling that after the holiday Mom would probably crash. Knowing my Mom, I figured she was holding on for Christmas and, after she made it through that, she would let go. She did. The Monday after New Year's Maria came and got me with the words "Teddy is dying." She was non-responsive and Maria couldn't rouse her. This was the first time she went down and really appeared to be dying. I called my brothers on the phone and we prepared for the worst. By the end of the day, however, she had bounced back and was talking, joking and seemed like her old self again. We didn't realize it at the time, but Mom was "stair-stepping" toward the end of her life. She would have these episodes, usually on a Monday or Tuesday, where she would crash and seem on the verge of dying and then, miraculously, come back. However, the 'back' was never as far back as she had been before—she was moving closer and closer to death.

It was at this time that Dave and I decided that we had better start going through her things *in earnest*. My mother was a saver. One might actually call her a hoarder, although not the kind of "you can't walk through the house except through a little path" type of hoarder (and I would never call her that, lol!). Having been a child when the Great Depression hit, I think she was scarred for life. So she saved things—everything—because you just never knew when you might need them, right? When Dave and I helped her pack up her house to move we thought we'd go through and purge a bunch of stuff that she hadn't used in years. Oh NO! She had a meltdown when I tried to do that. So, we just boxed everything up, moved it down and had been quietly letting stuff go over the years. Mostly the junk, like plastic bags, jars, canning material, things she had long ago forgotten about.

Now, however, it was time to start going through the personal stuff: the keepsakes and journals, diaries and mementos. Christmas cards, birthday cards, anniversary cards and mother's day cards, along with all the letters and pictures and memorabilia she had kept for the past 80 years. How could I possibly decide what to keep and what to discard? Well, it just had to be done. Dave and I anticipated that my brothers would want us to sell the house as soon as possible after my mother's death and they weren't around to help so it was time to open the boxes and see what was inside. We figured that when the time came, my portion of the sale might allow us to purchase *something*, but it would most likely be smaller than where we were currently living, so the plan was to pare down *our* stuff by at least one-third to one-half and only save the most precious things of my Mom's.

My advice to anyone doing this? It's much easier if the person is still alive and in the next room. Here we are, months after she passed, still going through her stuff. Somehow, having her in the next room made it easier to make decisions about everything as we opened one box after another, went through and decided who would get what and what would be tossed. Now, it's much more difficult to decide to let go of things…anything. However, it has to be done. My older brother just wanted us to throw everything away—at our last get-together he said, "Don't open the boxes. If you haven't looked at it in 17 years you won't miss it. Just toss it in the dumpster." It seemed heartless to me; and it was said with such anger. It was probably just his way of dealing with his grief. But one of the gems we found were the love letters my Dad sent to my Mom from before they were married and all throughout their marriage. What a find! If I had done what my brother wanted those would've been lost forever and we never would've known that my Dad was such a romantic.

The coolest thing we found was my Mom's life history. Unfortunately, it doesn't include the adventures she had with us, but Dave and I started reading it to her during the last few months of her life and it was SO GOOD for her: First, it helped ground her and helped her remember who she was and all the parts of her life that she had forgotten. There were many, many times that my Mom would get a panicky look on her face and exclaim, "I just don't know anything. I don't know who I am, I don't know! I don't know anything!" Either Dave or I would get the journal out and we'd start reading it (or sometimes we'd just start reciting her life history from memory) and soon she'd be back, remembering who she was and the events of her life that brought her to us. She'd calm down and be reassured that yes, in fact, she *did* remember who she was and the course of her life. Second, there were so many stories I had never heard about my Mom's life that I felt like I was getting to know her in such a different way – more of the teenaged her, the girl I could've been besties with in college, than the Mom she became to me. It felt like almost a cruel game to discover this person as she virtually disappeared before my eyes and yet I'm so glad I got to know the whole of my mother and not just the 'mom' part of her. I had hoped my brothers could share in this discovery, too, and I offered one of them the opportunity to read her history to her (at least parts of it) the last weekend he was here before she died. I'm not sure he read very much and I don't know if it had the same impact on him as it did on me. Unfortunately my younger brother never spent enough time with her to be able to read to her. And now, due to circumstances beyond my control, I'm not sure they'll ever get to read her history (more on that to come).

THE LAST FEW YEARS

Eight

Easter

The weekend before Easter a memorial service was planned for my uncle, Dick Bateman. Dick was my mother's brother-in-law. He had been married to her youngest sister, Lenore, who died of breast cancer two days after my father's death.

Interesting factoid: my mother dated Dick before they each married someone else. I think they went on a couple of dates before she found her sister, Lenore, sobbing in the basement of their home. When Mom asked her why she was so upset, Lenore told her that she was in love with Dick and thought Mom was heartless and cruel to be dating him. My mother had no idea her 15-year-old sister was in love (from afar) with someone she just happened to be dating, so she immediately stopped dating him. It wasn't long after that, Lenore and Dick started dating and, in fact, they actually got married before my Mom and Dad. All of us kids (hers included) got a kick out of the story.

Dick had been living in Fremont with his son and daughter-in-law, and the service would be held there. Dave and I really wanted to go. When we had been living at my parent's home in the Bay Area the year before we got married Dave had gotten close to Dick and Lenore and I had always been close to them – Lenore had treated me like the daughter she never had and I even made a film called *Reflections of a Life* which was inspired by her life and subsequent battle with breast cancer.

After some research, we discovered that hospice allowed for something they called respite care so we inquired to see if we could schedule that for Mom for the weekend so we could go up to Fremont to attend the memorial service. The answer was yes, we could schedule the respite care. However, because my mother could no longer feed herself, our attendant would need to work 8 hours per day at the nursing facility, attending to my mom and feeding her. So, she could stay at the facility (for free), but her care would have to be paid for by us. Hmm. Not exactly what we had hoped.

By this point in time all of my Mom's extra money had run out and, although we had appealed to my brothers to step up and help out by splitting the payment for her care three ways, they both declined. I don't know where they thought *we* were going to get the extra money—a money tree in the backyard, perhaps? We had interviewed a couple of other caretakers in the hopes of finding someone who could come in and take Maria's place for less money, but no one seemed as capable as Maria, and they didn't want to work for what we could afford. Finally, Maria came to us (after noticing that we had been interviewing others) and asked if she could help out. She offered to continue working for less and we accepted. We decided we were just going to have to get through it any way we could. However, the only way we could afford to have Maria work full time at the nursing facility over the weekend while we were gone, would be to *not* have her work during the following week for two days. So, that's what we did in order to go to Fremont to attend my uncle's service. I think my younger brother (who also attended) was as surprised to see us at the service as we were to see him. He was there with his friend and they didn't seem to want to hang out with us, so after the service they went off together and Dave and I went to visit my surrogate mother, Mary Jones, in Palo Alto.

When I was 8 years old my parents thought it would be nice for me to befriend a girl who had just moved into the neighborhood named Lisa. My parents knew her parents as my Dad had once dated her mother, a long, long time before (before either set of parents got married). When we heard that, we always teased them about it. But that's another story. My first remembrance of Lisa was when I saw her climb out of her bedroom window, which was on the front of their house, as my parents dropped me off at her house to attend her 8th birthday party. We became instant best friends and stayed that way all through grade school, junior high and high school. I spent as much time at her house as I did at my own and her mother was a second mother to me (as I believe mine was to her). Lisa's father died a couple of years prior to that time and I very much wanted to see her mother before it was too late. Since I almost never got up to the Bay Area anymore, I took this chance to find out where her mother was and went for a visit. Yes, Mary had aged (haven't we all?), but she was glad to see me and I, her. She lived in a beautiful assisted-living facility in Palo Alto and even though she was legally blind she still got around and had some independence, her own nice-sized room with amenities (and all her beautiful pictures of family on the wall) and seemed to be doing pretty well. She missed her husband, Cal, and spoke about wanting to join him soon. I'm sure she missed her daughter, Claudia, as well, who died of a very bad stroke a few years earlier. Claudia was the oldest in the family, while Lisa was the youngest.

When Dave and I got back we were able to bring Mom greetings from Mary, which warmed her heart. It was very, very difficult for Mom when we left her at the nursing facility. She cried every day, according to Maria, asking why she was there and when she could go home almost constantly. When I heard that, it broke my heart and I knew we would never do that again. We never did. I made sure my brothers knew how Mom reacted to being at the nursing facility as they had both pushed really hard to put Mom in a nursing home when her money ran out. Of course, someone would've had to pay for *that* until her long-term care policy kicked in (after the first 100 days) and nobody seemed to be able to afford to do that. So that was really no solution. I had told them that she vehemently did *not* want to go to a nursing home and that doing so would kill her.

They both poo-poo'd the idea, but I knew I was right.

A few days after we got back (and got Mom back home) her best friend, Zilpha, came to visit. Mom always loved these visits with Zilpha. They were so cute together. Zilpha was an awfully good friend to Mom. She visited her every day when Mom was recovering from her hip surgery in the rehab facility. They called each other "best friend" and every time Zilpha visited, Mom perked up. Even though she was now exhibiting signs of dementia and short term memory loss, she would remember these visits for quite some time afterward. Mom was usually sitting out in the front room, on her spot on the couch, when Zilpha would visit, but this time Mom was in bed, on oxygen, as this was about a week before she passed. Mom's breathing was labored, even at this point, and it troubled Zilpha. She asked us why we couldn't do anything about it. But there was really nothing we *could* do. It was just part of the process. The next week, when Zilpha called and asked if she could visit, I thought it best to say no. By that time Mom was non-responsive and her breathing was even worse and I knew it would be too distressing for Zilpha to see her like that. I was glad they had had such a nice visit the week before—it was a nice send-off for Mom.

I understood how hard it was for Zilpha. Back when my Dad was dying and I had gone to visit him the last weekend he was alive, I had hoped to visit my aunt Lenore, too. I knew she was probably near the end of her life, as well. My Mom called down to see if it was okay and Dick said no, she just wasn't well enough to receive visitors. I felt really, really sad that I didn't get a chance to go see her and say goodbye. Particularly when she died just two days later on Wednesday (that was a Monday). So, it was difficult for me to tell Zilpha, "no," when she asked to come and see Mom because I knew the feeling of being told "no" and knowing that you would never see that person again. It sucks. But Zilpha was about to turn 103 in a month and I didn't want to be the cause of her *not* making it to her birthday due to undue distress! I'm happy to say that Zilpha made it to 105 before she finally passed away peacefully in her sleep. She was quite depressed when my Mom passed, but she weathered it. The thing that upset her the most is how my brothers treated me, but I'm getting ahead of myself here.

Nine

Mother's Day

At one point, probably two to three weeks before her death, Mom asked Dave if she was dying. Poor Dave. Such a sweet soul. He just couldn't bear to admit to her (or himself for that matter) that yes, indeed, she was dying. So, he said "No, Mom, you've been living with us for 16 years and we'd love to have you with us for another 16, at least." After she passed, I thought back to that moment many times. I wondered if we had told her, "Yes, Mom, you are dying," would it have given her comfort in knowing what was coming and allowed her to accept the inevitable, not fight it so hard and make peace at the end? Or would it have scared her? Maybe even scared her into staying with us a little bit longer? I don't know. What I do know is as she was laying there, fighting so hard for life, heart beating strongly and struggling for each breath, there was a moment when I believe she realized that she, in fact, *was* dying. This was Wednesday afternoon, the day before she passed. I was standing next to her; the hospice attendant, the hospice nurse and Maria were all in the room with me. Mom was very agitated and very clearly cried out, "Help!" We all heard it. At the time I just reacted as I had in the past when she called out for help and told them that she often called out "help" when she felt the urge to go to the bathroom. I leaned in and reassured her that the nurses were there and she could let go and do whatever she needed to do and they would take care of her, clean it up and clean her. I didn't realize that her bladder and all functions had ceased by that time. As I thought about it later, I don't think she was calling for bathroom assistance. I think she was calling for someone to help her to *not die*. Perhaps, as she finally fully realized she was dying, she was afraid. She stayed very agitated for some time after that and, although I tried and tried to calm her, I just couldn't and I had to leave the room—it was just too difficult to see her like that. When I returned her eyes had closed, she was calmer and seemed to be sleeping. She never returned to consciousness until right before she passed.

About 10 days before my mother died the signs that she was heading in that direction were unmistakable. Dave and I decided we had better start making some final preparations and headed to a mortuary in Simi Valley that had been recommended by a friend. We knew this could be a complicated situation since she lived with us in Southern California but the burial would take place in Northern

California—that was where she and my father had purchased their plot together back in the 1980s. He was interred there in June of 1992 and the headstone was already engraved with my mother's name and birthdate...it was just waiting for her final death date. The man at the mortuary was very kind and their pricing was surprisingly reasonable...much more so than we anticipated. We chose a beautiful white casket for her with a spray of red and white roses, since red is her favorite color. The people at the mortuary would take care of all the arrangements, including transporting her to Skylawn Memorial Park in San Mateo. One more item checked off the list of to-do's.

Saturday, the day before Mother's Day, was the last day my Mom was somewhat alert and participating in life. My brother and his wife came into town that day and offered to take over some of our duties and let us go out and have a break, although by that time the duties were pretty light—Mom wasn't eating anymore, couldn't get out of bed to use the commode and was mostly sleeping. So, their real function was to sit with her and make sure that if the end was near that people were called. I think Dave gave my brother some chocolate ice cream to give to Mom and she may have eaten half a spoonful. But that was the last time, I believe, that she ate anything. And whether or not and for how long they actually sat with her? I have no idea. This was the first time Dave and I left the house together, without Mom (other than to attend my uncle's memorial), in years. Literally. By the time we got back my brother and sister-in-law were both in the other room, watching TV.

The next day was Sunday, Mother's Day. My younger brother came over, along with my niece and we all sat in Mom's room to keep her company. She was not responding at this point and seemed to be in a lot of pain, so morphine was administered to try and keep the pain level down. By the end of the day, when she was still alive, I was secretly glad that she didn't pass on *that* day. I didn't think I could bear it if my Mom passed on Mother's Day. Selfish, I know, but deep inside I still wanted her around for just *one more day*, even though it was obvious that she had one foot on the other side.

Monday morning. I hoped Maria, with her sunny disposition and her ability to get my Mom to eat and drink copious amounts, could lift her up from the jaws of death as she seemed to be able to do on previous occasions. But, alas, all her efforts seemed in vain this time. We sang "You Are My Sunshine" to my Mom, urging her to sing along by leaving out the ends of the verses, and she did her best to fill them in, but her voice was barely a whisper. She was just tired…so tired…and we decided it was time to call Hospice. The end was near. We called Mom's sister, Merlyn, in Utah and put the earbuds in Mom's ears so she could hear. Merlyn told her how much she loved her and what a great older sister she had been…how she had taken care of Merlyn and their younger sister, Lenore (who had already passed), like she was their mother, and that Merlyn was always grateful for that. Mom was able to croak out "I love you" to her sister. I hope she heard it and understood the effort it took for Mom to say those words. Those were the last words she actually spoke other than calling for help.

I took one last selfie with my Mom. She didn't look as

good as I wanted, but it's the last picture I have of her and I'll treasure it forever. "This is really it," I thought. I guess I had hoped, in my heart of hearts, that she had just stair-stepped down a little and would rally again, like she had in the past. But Mondays were when she always rallied and she didn't this time. I had to face the fact that my mom was really and truly going to die. Maybe tomorrow. Definitely in the next day or two. It wasn't like I hadn't known this, intellectually, all along. She had been in hospice since late December. But knowing it and *really knowing it* are two different things, I guess. I had said everything I needed to say. I think she had, too. Now it was just time for her to let go and step into the next adventure.

Tuesday I spent the day sitting with my Mom. It wasn't easy as every breath was a struggle and it broke my heart that she was working so hard to stay alive. I wanted her to just rest and pass in peace. Of course, I didn't *want* her to die but, knowing that this would be the final outcome, I wanted it to be easy for her. I had heard stories about people just going to sleep and never waking up. It seemed so peaceful. Why couldn't it be that way for my Mom, too? Unfortunately, it was not to be for her. She would fight it all the way to the end. The will to live was strong with her.

The hospice nurse came that afternoon and decided that indeed the end was near and scheduled round-the-clock hospice care to begin that night at 8 pm. They broke out the end-of-life kit from the refrigerator, started Mom on the Ativan and upped the dosage of the morphine. I didn't realize that these drugs would now make my Mom unavailable to me – she would basically disappear into a drugged-out haze for the rest of her life as she struggled to breathe and hang on 'for dear life.' The vigil now began in earnest.

I asked my husband, after this whole thing was over, if the drugs were really necessary. I know that she was in pain, I could see it on her face, and I didn't want her to be in pain, obviously, so administering the morphine for the pain seemed necessary (at least in the smaller amounts that they started with). However, it also seems to me that, as the medical professionals believe the end is near, the dosages become larger and larger, almost as if they are helping with the process. This is the part I wonder about. But then again, if we let nature take its course would that really be humane? I don't know. I just know that having my Mom lay there, drugged out and struggling for every breath, seemed not so great to me.

Dying from old age is, apparently, quite different from dying of an illness or a terminal disease. According to the hospice nurse there is a course to death and when you have a terminal disease that course is followed almost like a script, and they can pretty much predict when a person will pass. But when a person is dying from old age the process can be unpredictable and can take much, much longer. The body is basically 'giving up' and it gives up in stages. We had seen this with my Mom over the course of the previous 6 months. The Monday after New Years was the first time. Each time she had one of the episodes where she looked like it was the end, she never fully recovered and we knew she was 'stair-stepping' toward the inevitable final passing. This time, however, it was THE final passing. She would not come back from this.

The nurses told me that, as a person is dying, the sense of hearing is the last to go. One of the first things to go is the ability to speak. Interesting. I wondered how they would know this. Anyway, I decided I would try and make my Mom's transition as peaceful and easy as possible. We played lovely classical music—her favorite—and I spoke to her of my love for her and of all the people who were patiently (or impatiently) waiting just on the other side: her own mother and father, her sisters, her brother, my dad. I hoped this would help alleviate any fears she might have and let her know that she was loved both here and there.

I had a sense that she was experiencing 'the call' from the other side for weeks, even months, before she passed as she would dream very vivid dreams about her parents. She would wake up in the middle of the night or early in the evening after a nap and need desperately to go home. The 'home' she was referring to was where she grew up. At these times she seemed not to know who I was. One day when Maria had her sitting outside on the front porch to get some sun she asked about the 'lady in the white dress' standing there, which freaked Maria out a little bit since they were the only two present. Mom pointed and said there was "a lady in a long white dress standing there." Maria was convinced it was an angel coming to check up on my Mom to see if she was ready yet.

Ten

The Last Day

Early Thursday morning the Hospice nurse came to check on my Mom again. "She is so strong," she said. "That's my Mom." "It will probably be somewhere between 12-24 hours." My husband slept a little in the bed in her room while I sat with her. The hospice attendant sat in the room. Maria hovered nearby. Then Maria and the hospice attendant went into the kitchen and chatted quietly. I sat with Mom, held her hand and started to tell her what a wonderful life she had led. I wanted her to know that she could leave without any regrets—

that she had done everything she had ever wanted to do. Maybe she hadn't done it immediately, when she first thought she would, but she had been able to do everything she wanted to do: travel, get her college degree, raise 3 children and adopt and raise a 4th, get to know 3 grandchildren and a great-grandchild, enjoy playing golf and bridge, be a professional actress, be a good friend to many, many people and much, much more. I told her how much I loved her and when I said that she actually opened her eyes, looked at me and tears rolled down her cheeks. I could see that she was trying to speak. So I told her that I knew that she loved me, too. Dave, listening quietly there, thanked me for enumerating all of her accomplishments and letting her know what a wonderful life she led and then he, too, left the room and my Mom and I were completely alone.

I leaned in close and said, somewhat conspiratorially, "You can let go. I will be okay. I will miss you terribly but I will be okay." I said a few more things that, for now, I will leave as private last words between her and me. But almost as soon as I finished I felt the struggle cease. She took another couple of breaths and then she let go. The effort to hang onto life stopped. The breathing stopped. I knew immediately that her spirit had left her body. Being with her in that moment when she passed from this life to the next was the most sacred moment I have ever experienced.

I have only had this experience one other time and it was with Dave's sister, Kathy. She died from AIDs-related complications and was surrounded by her sisters, mother, Dave and myself—a virtual ring of love in her hospital room. This was the same but different. It was just my Mom and I. Alone together. Maybe she wanted it that way—just the two of us. Maybe this was the way she experienced my birth. I don't know—I've never had children. But it was beautiful… heartbreaking and yet peaceful all at the same time.

I waited a minute or two to savor the moment, telling myself it was just to be sure that she would not take another breath. I knew she wouldn't. She had finally let go. Truthfully, I didn't want to break the spell of the moment. But, ultimately, I needed to let someone know. So I walked to the next room to get the hospice attendant and Maria. Dave heard me tell them I thought she had stopped breathing and came as well. And the circus called death began.

First, they called the hospice nurse, who needed to make her determination before the Doctor would be called to the house to make the final pronouncement. They then called the funeral home to come and get her. Before they could leave, the next step was to go through her medications and paraphernalia, deciding what to take and what to dispose of. It took about an hour before they were finally done and, after signing the paperwork, they left just as the funeral home arrived. The attendants wrapped the body in their sheets and blankets, giving me (and Maria and Dave if we wanted) time alone with the body to say our last goodbyes before covering her face and taking her out to the hearse. It was all, finally, over. I paid Maria her final check and she left, never to return. At that moment the house felt strangely empty and quiet. No breathing machine. No Maria. No nurses. Yet, I could still feel my mother's presence in that room.

And no, I didn't cry. Not when she passed. Not when the doctor came and made the pronouncement and not when the funeral home came and gave us our last moments with the body. Not even when they drove away and I knew I would never see her again. But I did feel the heavy weight of grief descend around me after everyone was gone – it was crushing.

It was all truly over and yet, in many ways, it was just beginning.

Eleven

The Funeral

The funeral. I had an idea what my mother would want. And yet... I guess I was in shock and overwhelm. My brothers seemed to be the same as they were of no help at all. So, okay. Plan a program. It should be easy, right? I had a couple of programs of other funerals my husband and I had performed at in recent months. Yes, we 'perform' at funerals. A bit weird, I know.

My husband and I met singing together in a band. It wasn't my band and it wasn't his, either. The name of the band was Scott McKuen & Company. We were "& Company." I was the last to join. They were actually looking to have 4 members: 2 men and 2 women. Scott and David were the two men and once I joined they were going to look for another woman but they just never got around to it and that was that. As we prepared for upcoming gigs it became clear why: David and I were the musicians of the group and Scott just sort of went along with whatever we proposed. My background in music (I was a child prodigy on the piano and spent years performing recitals and concerts before becoming a piano major in college) made me the one who actually wrote the arrangements down. Dave's background in music (he was a child performer on the USO circuit) made him the one who often initiated the arrangements. I filled in the harmonies.

When Scott got hepC and couldn't perform we re-arranged the songs for 2-part harmony and kept the group going until it became clear that we would be better off just forming a duo. Oh, and did I mention we were starting to fall in love? Cut to many years later, we were known as the resident music people in our local church—the one's who could be called upon in a pinch to do weddings, funerals and the like. Usually Dave would sing and I would accompany him on the piano.

I thought it would be nice to honor my mother by having the family participate on the program but my brothers were really loath to take part in any meaningful way. Neither one wanted to speak. Finally one agreed to give a prayer. He offered that his daughter might sing a song and his wife gave another prayer. That was the extent of the family participation and it became what my husband and I lovingly refer to as the 'Kathi & Dave show.' Dave sang a song (and I accompanied him), I gave the eulogy, or life sketch as I called it and my niece sang (and I accompanied her, too). We asked a former Bishop from our church to give a talk. Dave edited together an amazing memorial video, set to beautiful music, which memorialized and represented the fullness of my mother's life. We spent hours poring through thousands of pictures in order to fully represent her lifelong pursuits, joys, high points and passions, staying up 'til the wee hours of the morning every night right up until the night before the actual service. I found out later that my brothers and nephew went to a baseball game that night. I know people process grief in different ways but somehow that just hit me wrong. This was their mother. I wished they could've somehow spent more time honoring her and the life she gave them.

No sooner did we arrive back home from the luncheon (which followed the funeral) then we packed our bags and headed up to the San Francisco Bay area for the interment, which was to be held at 1:00 the next day. I left the planning of that up to my younger brother and his friend who lives in San Jose. Supposedly announcements were made in the church up there where my Mom had some friends who were still alive, but only two of her good friends were able to make it to the graveside service: Janet Leonard and JoAnn Rogers. I was so glad to see Janet, who had known my Mom since before we were born (she drove my Mom to the hospital to have one of us kids—I just don't remember which one). I know Mom would have been happy to see her and Jo there—we had my parents' 25th wedding anniversary party at JoAnn's place.

For as long as I can remember my parents had always teased us that we would have to give them a great, big 25th wedding anniversary party. Of course, when both my brother and I were away at college that year, I think they decided they would give us a pass. So, imagine their surprise when we both came home in March for the weekend and, unbeknownst to them, had planned this big surprise shindig at their friends' house. Every one of their brothers and sisters, my Dad's mother and a bunch of their good friends were all on the guest list, none of whom had spilled the beans beforehand, and they all were there and yelled "surprise!" at the appropriate moment. Let me tell you it took no small amount of planning to make that happen, especially since it was my first year away at college. I had to plan that party long-distance with JoAnn (this was before cell phones and email after all, which meant lots of letter-writing because long-distance calls were *expensive* for a college student). The look of surprise on both my Mom and Dad's faces when they walked through that door and saw all their friends and family there? Priceless!

Yes, having JoAnn and Janet witness my Mom reach her final resting place would've meant a lot to her. Lo and behold, when the time came my brothers stood up and decided to say a few words. They *wanted* to participate? I was gobsmacked, to say the least. Hmm. Okay, I guess they decided not to let *every* opportunity pass to pay tribute to her. I, too, stood up and said a few words myself, although I didn't recite the entire eulogy. I tried to give the spirit of my sketch, without reading the entire thing. Lunch afterward in Redwood City was a nice affair and we all got to visit, watch the video and remember Mom.

Dave and I decided to stay an extra day in the Bay Area.

THE LAST FEW YEARS

We were just exhausted after everything—the funeral(s), the years spent caring for my Mom and the stress of it all—we were totally physically and emotionally spent. We picked a hotel online and pretty much crashed. There was an HBO movie playing that night starring Bryan Cranston that I wanted to see so I watched it as Dave went out and got us pizza. Darned if the first song they played over the closing credits wasn't "Don't Fence Me In." It was almost as if my Mom was telling me she was okay—she was free and independent again and I didn't need to worry. The next morning as I was getting dressed and ready to go what should I hear from the TV in the next room? "Don't Fence Me In" playing over some commercial for the Nevada Tourism board. I tell you, I have never, and I mean *never* in all my years in the business of film and television, heard that song used in any film or TV show and here it was on TV twice in less than 12 hours. Right after we buried my mother? Too much of a coincidence for me. Even my husband, Dave, who doesn't go in much for the woo-woo thought it was kinda strange... in a good way.

Twelve

The Aftermath

Here's where things got interesting. First, Dave and I decided that the weekend after the two funeral services, which happened to be the Memorial Day Holiday, we would take a vacation. It was the first vacation we had taken together in probably 8 years, due to my Mom's health…and boy did we need it. We were, frankly, exhausted—both physically and emotionally—from everything. Those of you reading this who have been caretakers or who *are* caring for someone who is terminally ill know it is not an easy task, and it is often thankless work. Hours upon hours of personal hygiene, feeding, trying to keep their spirits up (and your own as well), all while fighting your own emotions of frustration, grief, anger, sadness and overwhelm over the changes that have and are taking place in your loved one, their inability to interact with you in the same way they once did, as well as their inability to do the simplest tasks. You're constantly keeping your own emotions in check because you don't want to upset the patient—they can't help the changes that have overtaken their body—and yet the emotions that you're feeling are very real and you have no outlet for them.

At the same time, any attempt to do some of the simplest things: like laundry, house cleaning, dishes, things that most people take for granted, can feel like overwhelming tasks--these things often fall by the wayside, or at least get done in a very haphazard way. So, our attempt to clean house? Well, that had gone out the window quite some time earlier, particularly in the midst of trying to go through some of my Mom's boxes and things. It was at this time that I got a call from my brother wherein he stated that he and my other brother had been talking about how they wanted to approach selling the house (hmm, where were WE in this discussion, I wondered). He then informed me that he had set up a visit with his realtor for the following Saturday at 1:00 p.m. As you might imagine, I blew a gasket.

Now, understand that we had just returned from our 3-day weekend away when I got this call and *that* weekend had happened on the heels of returning from the service in the Bay Area. The house was a wreck and he was, literally, giving us 3 days to put it into pristine, showcase, show-the-realtor condition. Um…no. Not possible. I read him the riot act and told him in no uncertain terms would his realtor be coming to our home in 3 days. If HE wanted to come and help us go through Mom's things, he was welcome to do so. But he needed to chill out and wait a bit before making an appointment to show the house. So, after some grousing, both of my brothers came that Saturday, at about 1:00 pm, and helped Dave put a few things in the dumpster and then promptly sat and watched TV for the rest of the day. They didn't come back for two weeks, which was when they scheduled the realtor to come back.

I was already a little peeved with my brother regarding this particular realtor—my brother started pushing us to have that realtor come out in January, six months earlier. I distinctly remember this because it happened right around the time I was scheduled to go to Sundance (Sundance Film Festival). I almost *didn't* go to Sundance because that was the first time Mom did her 'stairstep' and I didn't want to be gone if she was going to pass away. However, she recovered and it appeared that she was doing okay so I went ahead and made the trip, although I cut it to five days instead of seven (which is short because Sundance goes for ten days). At that time my brother was pushing us to contact his realtor and, when we finally did, the realtor started pushing us to let him come over and list the house. I finally had to let my brother know that his guy was too pushy and wanted to list the house right then and there. Really? Talk about premature—Mom wasn't dead yet.

So, okay. If it was time for my brother's realtor to see the house, then I figured let's let them *all* in on the action. I set up a Saturday extravaganza where my brother's realtor, our realtor (the one who sold us the house in the first place) and a third realtor (one recommended by the Trustee) would all come to the house, all do evaluations of the property and all give their recommendations. As I suspected, they all pretty much said the same thing and, unlike what my brother was hoping, they didn't get into a 'competition' with each other and drop their rate. Hah! I knew *that* wasn't going to happen. That extra two weeks also gave Dave and me time to fill 3 dumpsters and get the place in shape to be seen by people who would be evaluating it and deciding what kind of a price they would put on it.

After the realtors all left, it was the Trustee's turn to do *his* thing. Many years prior, about a year after she bought the house, my mother had decided to put the house in a trust. This was done so that when she passed it would not, technically, be part of her 'estate' and be subject to estate taxes, but would pass through the trust to the successor beneficiaries. Initially she was the only beneficiary of the trust and she passed her beneficial interest to my two brothers and myself in shares. She happened to meet the man who would put the trust together, and who would become the Trustee, at a Christmas party that Dave and I had at the end of the first year that we lived in the house. Totally on her own, and unbeknownst to me, she engaged him in a conversation after she overheard him talking about the fact that he was in the business of creating trusts. Apparently she was satisfied with what she heard and decided to hire him to create her trust. Several years later, in 2006, she decided to amend the trust and change the division of the beneficial interest. When the trustee came to the house to do that, he asked Dave to set up a camera and record the conversation he had with her. That conversation lasted about an hour. So, that Saturday after all the realtors left, we all watched that DVD and then he passed out copies of the Trust Indenture. I needed to excuse myself to the girl's room for a few minutes and when I got back both my brothers were gone. I asked the Trustee where they were and he said that they had gotten up and left without a word, taking their copies of the trust with them. They have never spoken to me again. I mean – I have not seen or heard from them since that day—I didn't know it at the time but my brothers severed all relations with me at that moment.

Before they left, it had been decided that, whatever happened and whichever realtor was chosen, we were going to try and list and sell the house as quickly as possible. The target date my brothers wanted was July 15. Since it was around June 15 that we were having that discussion, and Dave and I were going to be doing all of the work of packing up my mother's things (as well as our own), I urged a later date—perhaps the first or second week in August. Besides that, there were things that we felt should or could be done to improve the value of the house and therefore the sales price. Once my brothers left, however, we were on our own to decide whether or not we should make any necessary repairs, who would pay for them, and when they were 'expecting' the house to be ready. In other words, everything was up in the air, as far as we knew. Also, incidentally, in the terms of the Trust as set forth by my Mom, she wanted me to stay, or to be able to stay in the house, and she structured it so that I could 'buy out' my brothers' interest, which definitely threw a monkey wrench in the plans… at least their plans for a quick sale and cash out.

So, we set about trying to pack up the house as quickly as possible. However, since it was a 3300 square foot house, and we were packing all of our own personal items, Dave's business *and* going through all of my mother's things, my father's things and all of my brothers' things (and deciding what to keep, what to discard and who would get what) it ended up being a monumental task. An emotional one, as well.

As time wore on it ultimately became clear that I would not hear from my brothers nor would they help us go through my mother's personal effects, many of which happened to be theirs or were things I thought they'd like to have. I had hoped that they would blow off some steam and then come back so that we could discuss whatever was bothering them. But that was never to be.

I could, of course, try to figure out or assume what they were thinking and why they decided never to contact us again. But why? It was just too much emotional energy at a time when I was already spending too much emotional energy packing up my life and my mother's life. I decided if that's who they were, then I no longer needed them in my life. Boy was I right!

Then along came the lawsuit. I know you're scratching your head and thinking…lawsuit?! Yep. Lawsuit. Cue record screetch here.

The sad thing is this: at the time that they filed their lawsuit, along with their *lis pendens* (a legal document that is basically a lien against the property), we had two pending offers on the house. So, in fact, we had packed up and cleaned up the house and gotten it into a satisfactory condition so the Trustee could get busy like a little bee and try to sell the place. The idea of cutting off your nose to spite your own face is appropriate here. This was, unfortunately, not the first time they did something really stupid with regard to this estate. [Note: one of those offers was substantially the same as what the house ultimately sold for a year and a half later, although when the house sold we had all accrued attorneys' fees, and the realtor deducted an extra amount for "fixing up the house" so there was, essentially, far less in the estate to split at that point.]

Oh, and the Trustee had made them an offer. Even though they were not in contact with me, they had sent several letters to the Trustee and the last one had threatened a lawsuit. With that in mind, he had offered to compromise, meaning change the percentages that my mother had clearly outlined in her Trust. They said they were open to that. So he put together an offer, which we felt, and he felt, was a fair offer, given the division that my mother had specified in the Trust. Technically he did *not* have to consult us with regard to any offer he might make, but he did so in order to assure himself that we would approve it should they accept it. We approved it. However, their answer was to have their attorney file the lawsuit and the Trustee never heard from them directly again, either.

You can guess where it went from there. Yep, it got ugly.

Thirteen

The Lawsuit

Let me start here by saying that this wasn't all quite as simple as I'm painting it. Being sued by your own brothers is as horrifying as you might expect, especially when you thought you were close. This kind of betrayal cuts deep. I spent days crying myself to sleep and feeling the kind of despair and depression I've only felt a few times in my life. I think the only thing that actually saved me was the spirit of my sweet mother who came to me, in my darkest moments, reassuring me that everything would turn out okay and that she was there, with me, to see this through. Even as I thought to myself "How could they do this to me, their own sister?" I knew, somewhere deep inside, that what had motivated them *to do* this was the same thought, "How could she do this to us, her own brothers?" The only difference was the fact that I actually *hadn't done anything* to them.

There had been precious few communications between my brothers and the Trustee once they left the house that day in June. One was a letter, addressed to the Trustee, that was sent by my older brother about 2-3 weeks after the meeting. In it they referred to me and my husband as "The Tenants" and demanded that we pay rent to the tune of $10,000 per month while we were going through my mother's things and closing up the house. If I hadn't figured it out prior to that, this made it very clear that their primary interest in my mother's estate was money. It was almost funny for a couple of reasons: (1) no homes in that neighborhood were renting for anywhere near that price; and (2) my mother's home had some serious situations that needed addressing before it would be "up to code" for rental purposes, all of which we had outlined when we had our meeting and discussed the stuff we thought we should 'fix up' before we put the house up for sale. I suppose the implication was that we were to fix those items, pay for them ourselves, and then pay the rental to my brothers. Um, no. If we *were* going to pay any sort of rent, the renters (meaning us) would be reimbursed for any repairs, the rent thereafter would go to *the estate* and would be split in the proportions my mother outlined in her Trust, which meant the lion's share would come back to me anyway.

My brother then reached out to me by email a couple of months later to try and set up a meeting between the three of us to settle the thing 'amicably,' although I have my doubts about just how amicable it would have been. He made sure to insist that the Trustee *not* be included at that meeting, which I thought a bit strange. I agreed to meet, but since he went to extraordinary lengths in the email to let me know just how upset and 'livid' my younger brother was about the whole situation I wanted him to know that I was upset and hurt, as well. I also wanted him to know that I wasn't going to let the two of them gang up on me and have him, in the guise of being the mediator, *force* their agenda on me and bully me like they had been trying to do since my mother went into hospice. Especially since he was trying to assert himself as though he was still a lawyer and I had other, more recent information. Oh yes, I let him know that I would be putting all the cards on the table and letting our younger brother know all the less-than-favorable information I had discovered about him in the intervening months, including his bankruptcy, the foreclosure of his home and the fact that he had been disbarred from the practice of law because he had stolen a felonious amount of money from a client. Apparently he didn't like that and he cancelled the meeting.

A few weeks later their attorney struck the first blow, like a bully, with a letter that, basically, tried to extort a settlement from me by threatening to file their action if I didn't accept their terms. He also attached their 'Petition' so I could read what he was about to file to let me know he really meant business. Their 'action' included false charges against me of 'elder abuse,' coercion and collusion, amongst other things. My attorneys later described this Petition as including everything… including the kitchen sink.

Now, I'm not a lawyer. My Dad was a lawyer and my brother *was* a lawyer. My sister-in-law is also a lawyer. I have been around lawyers my entire life. I have worked for lawyers *a lot*. My very first job was subbing for my Dad's secretary when she went on summer vacation. I even defended myself, *in pro per*, in a lawsuit brought by a former client who had some hot shot entertainment attorney, and we went all the way to trial. Contrary to the opinion of my attorney brother and the caution by the Judge, who reminded me that if I lost even one of the 10 counts against me, I would lose, I won. On every count. Nevertheless, I did not feel comfortable taking on the defense of a probate case. This felt different to me. So we needed to hire a probate attorney. We called around for a referral and got one. Our referral was apparently to one of the best probate attorneys in town—a partner at a big downtown law firm who happens to now be a judge. She and her associate met with me (and Dave) and she looked over the case and we outlined everything. They spent a lot of time with us, asked a lot of questions, and decided to take on our case. However, their retainer was $20,000. Not a tiny fee. And we had to act fast as the first court date was right around the corner.

So, Dave and I put our heads together, prayed a lot and were able to borrow the money for the retainer. In hindsight, we wondered if my brothers had had similar conversations with their attorney. They knew we had asked them to help pay for

Mom's care during the last 6 months of her life. They refused. They had some erroneous idea that we were "living off" my mother or that we were "living in the house for free" and we wondered if their attorney didn't front-load the Petition with everything ("kitchen sink" our attorneys called it) to scare me into settling the case before it ever went anywhere. Maybe they thought we wouldn't have the wherewithal to hire an attorney ourselves and pay the retainer. I almost laughed out loud when we hatched that theory. Did my brothers not know me at all? Did they think they could accuse me of all sorts of heinous, false things, especially when it came to our mother, and I would just roll over? Um… no. Not me.

It was time to hit back with a definitive blow from our side to let them know that this kind of bullying would not be tolerated. Once I read their Petition, I finally understood what it was they thought I *had* done and, of course, I understood their anger at me. But the problem here was that I hadn't done any of the things they thought I had. A simple conversation, with open minds where they actually asked questions and listened to the answers, would have told them that. Unfortunately, they never gave me the benefit of the doubt and we never actually had that conversation.

So, that was that: I was accused, tried and found guilty without knowing what the charges were or being able to face my accusers and answer for myself. I found this to be hardly fair, given that we were blood. But, so be it. An interesting side note: as my husband and I went through the appalling probate litigation and mentioned it to friends it became clear that this is not a rare occurrence in this country. Apparently many, many people go through this even when there are valid wills and trusts in place (as in our situation). My guess is that when large sums of money are involved a couple of things occur: (1) people get greedy and start making up stories in their head about their siblings and other family members in order to justify grasping for what is not rightfully theirs (or what has not been left to them by the deceased); or (2) money-grubbing attorneys play on feelings of hurt and injury and 'stoke the fire' if you will, letting those who are feeling damaged, resentful and 'left behind' know that they can challenge the will or trust documents now that the person who created them has died and that the Court has no choice but to hear their challenge. Ultimately, regardless of how valid anyone's claims are (or aren't), the Court has to consider them and, as things often go, it's less expensive and time consuming to settle or go through mediation. That path leaves little for the parties who were supposed to inherit anything from the estate and much for the attorneys, though, and ends up being the worst possible path for those who are left behind. It is, however, the best possible path for the attorneys as they usually take the bulk of the estate through their legal fees. A win/win for them and a lose/lose for the survivors.

A word about 'elder abuse.' Apparently there are many different forms of this, legally. The type of elder abuse that I was being accused of was financial elder abuse. They insinuated that once we moved in together, I seized control of my mother's assets and money and held on with an iron fist, taking her money for my own benefit—living off of her, coercing her to leave the bulk of her estate to me, things like that. Now, my mother was a sweet woman but she was no pushover. The funny thing is, if my brothers gave it half a thought, they knew that. Their claim in their filing that my mother was some wilting flower who knew nothing about money or financial things was, in and of itself, laughable. She put herself (and my father) through school, *law* school at Stanford, working as a *bookkeeper* and once they married she took over handling all the family finances—budgeting, paying the bills, etc. In fact, my parents owned a vacation home in Northern California that they sold shortly before my father died. My parents 'took back' the loan themselves (essentially acting as the bank), and allowed the buyers to make the payments to them. This continued several years into the time my mother and I lived together. I knew, peripherally, that she was receiving a monthly check from the buyers of that house but it wasn't until after she died and I was going through her things that I realized that my mother kept a detailed ledger where she calculated the monthly payments, with amortized interest, until the balance was paid off. She calculated all this without the aid of a computer! She knew more about money than I did!

A note about my brothers' claim that, once we moved in together, we were living 'off of my mother' and that she was paying all of our expenses – essentially that my husband and I 'lived in the house for free.' Hah! My mother could barely afford to pay her own expenses *before* she moved in with us. Unfortunately, in this country, senior citizens who are living on Social Security often live below the poverty level. My mother, who grew up during The Great Depression, had money-handling skills that rivaled anybody out there, but even *she* was put to the test in her ability to live on a fixed income in Silicon Valley, as we later found out after we pieced things together. Her Social Security income, added to the amount she received from the vacation house they sold, didn't *quite* add up to what she needed each month in living expenses so she just ate less and less healthy foods than she should have. What *that* led to was a stint in the hospital and a diagnosis of chronic pancreatitis shortly after she moved in with us. The monthly expenses of the house in Southern California were about three times those of her house in Northern California. There was no way she could afford to pay those expenses all by herself. Again, my brothers were just making stuff up.

Of course, once she moved in with us we commenced paying for all of her monthly expenses – food, utilities, insurance – whatever was needed to make her comfortable and make sure she never worried about money again. In fact, it was our agreement to do so—she bought the house (for cash, from the proceeds of the sale of my childhood home in order to avoid a giant capital gains tax hit) and we would pay all of her living expenses in lieu of rent. It was an honor, as her daughter, to finally see her relax and start to enjoy life instead of always worrying about how she was going to meet the next month's bills. So the accusation that we somehow took advantage of her, financially, was ludicrous to me. My attorneys agreed. They went so far as to state that no judge would believe that we somehow conceived of a 'long con' wherein we would convince my Mom to let us live with her, take care of her for 16-1/2 years, pay all her expenses and sacrifice the last 3 years of our lives taking constant, round-the-clock care of her, just so we could maybe get a couple hundred thousand more out of her estate. It just seemed unbelievable to them.

The whole lawsuit thing just hurt me more than make me angry. That they would resort to taking this fight to the court system instead of coming to me and trying to work it out, between us, cut so deep. I understood that they were hurt: their mother left them less in her estate than she did me. They didn't understand why and she was no longer here to explain herself. So, in their 'not understanding' they decided it must not have been her intent *at all*. It must have been me. I must have done it. I must have coerced her into doing it because, on her own, she would never have done that. But what they didn't understand, and never let me explain, is that I had no idea that she had set things up this way in the first place. I could never have coerced this because I didn't know about it. So, in fact, she obviously had a reason for what she did and I can only imagine what that might have been.

Knowing my mother the way I did, and knowing that she wanted to be fair with all of her children, I have to think that her decision was based on a couple of things: first, the fact that she had been sending my older brother large sums of money over a long period of time (about 8 or 9 years that I can determine) that totaled in the neighborhood of $100,000, none of which had he ever paid back; and second, the fact that Dave and I had been taking care of her since my father died, first helping her with her previous home (in Northern California) and now paying all her living expenses in this one. It hadn't been *that* long since my mother cared for my father in his final illness and she knew what a toll that took on her so I imagine that she may have been thinking ahead to what we might encounter in caring for her in her final year or years of life. Of course, if she *was* thinking about that, she would've been right—taking care of her in those last few years was not easy. Yes, it was rewarding, but as we were doing it, it definitely took a toll on us, both physically and emotionally.

Interestingly, in the course of the litigation, it came out that my older brother *did* see the Trust and speak with my mother about it in 2002, shortly after she created it in 2001. Now, at the time he was a practicing attorney, with a specialty in estate law, so it is quite curious that if there were technical defects in the trust (as he claimed in the lawsuit), why he didn't mention anything about them at that time. Also, I have to wonder whether or not he asked my mother about the uneven distribution of the estate. Obviously since we were on opposite sides of this litigation I couldn't ask him if she told him anything at the time. So, it appears that the only people in the world who *might* know why my mother created the trust in the way she did was *her* and my brother, who won't tell anyone at this point because it isn't in his best interest to do so.

One of the hardest things of any litigation (and again, this wasn't the first one I had experienced) is the time. Things grind through the court system very, very slowly. Apparently, in probate matters, that time is even slower, by another 1/3. So a case that would normally take about a year in civil court takes about a year and a half in probate court. All along the way the attorneys are conferring, filing paperwork, doing discovery, and generating bills that would, to put it mildly, make your hair curl. As it went along, my husband and I started to get the feeling that my brothers' attorney was doing things and handling things in a way to create more work for my attorneys so that it would cost us the maximum amount of money. Now, I can't say for sure that this was their tactic, but it did start to feel like their ploy was to outmaneuver us by trying to force us to spend money on this case to the point where we would give up because it just cost too much.

For instance in December, shortly after they filed their action, all the attorneys agreed that it would be prudent to try and settle the action, especially since the estate was small enough that to go all the way through to a trial would decimate it, with most of the money going to the attorneys. So, to that end, their attorney agreed to draft a settlement. What this did was to put 'off calendar' the hearing that was scheduled for the first week in January until sometime in April. Great! However, the 'settlement proposal' that their attorney prepared wasn't offered up until the middle of February, even though the date on it (the date of preparation) was the middle of December. The 'settlement proposal' that they offered wasn't really a settlement proposal at all. No. It was a proposal of how the house would be sold and in it, they held out for the possibility that we would continue litigating the distribution of the assets all the way through to a trial. So, they wanted to force me out of the house but have the option to continue to litigate the facts of the case without any 'settlement' at all.

As another example, we ended up not settling before our paperwork was due for the April hearing. So next we went into what's called Discovery. This means questions are posed, formally, in writing (and required to be answered) and documentary evidence is required to be produced on both sides. However, before discovery started we had agreed to mediation (which is a settlement conference with a retired judge) and my attorneys thought that there was the chance that they would want to save money and *not* go through the expense of formal discovery process before mediation. But no, they served discovery on me. So, we served discovery on them, too. Their attorney seemed so anxious to get to this process—he wanted to SEE the documents that I had referenced in my Creditor's Claim…all the documentary evidence of the payments we had made throughout the years for repairs and improvements on the home, as well as the care of my mother. But after we filed our paperwork they never asked to see the documents. So, not so anxious to actually 'see' anything after all. Just anxious, it seems, to have me jump through the hoops and spend the money necessary to file the paperwork and respond to his.

Oh, I guess I should mention that the $20,000 retainer we gave our attorneys to hire them was kept "on file" and that we received bills from them each month for their time. Those bills ranged from $7500 to $30,000, depending on how much time they spent that previous month on our case. As long as the month wasn't too busy and the bills stayed in the $7500-$18,000/month range we were able to keep up. I know you're thinking… how? How could you do that? As I write this I'm wondering the same question myself. I know I had some money squirreled away and it's all gone now. All. Gone. Savings? Gone. And somehow the workload expanded into bigger, more profitable projects that helped pay these expanding bills. Whew!!

The mediation process was, to put it mildly, interesting. The mediator, a retired judge, would come into the room and tell us just how bad our case was—all the flaws and weak points. And then he would leave. And he would be gone for a long, long time. Now, as the mediation went on, it became clear that this was a negotiating tactic—he would tell us how awful our case was in order to get us to move off of our position and, I believe, he would then go into the room with my brothers and would tell them how bad their case was in order to move them off of their position. I understood the moves. It made sense to me. What was interesting was how *much* time he was spending with them versus how little time he was spending with us. Also, what was shocking to me was the absolute, unadulterated hate that was communicated, through him, from my brothers. I understood that they were hurt, angry even. But hate? That caught me off guard.

By days' end (and it really was a long day – about 11 hours) we arrived at a settlement. The mediator himself said, at one point, that he didn't believe it would happen. We compromised quite a bit. I'm sure they feel the same. My attorney said that both parties would leave unhappy and I'm sure she was right.

An agreement was written up, signed by everyone and it was time to gather our things to go home. Except, not quite. We had brought some things from the house for my brothers. As we had been going through stuff and packing up the house and my mother's things, we had found a number of personal items that belonged to either one or the other of my brothers, or items that either one of them had mentioned an interest in. As we came across these things, we put them in boxes, labeled with their names. We had about 6 of these boxes. We brought them to the mediation and Dave went to the car, with their attorney, off-loaded the boxes and told their attorney that it was all for them. However, when we returned to our car some time later (to give them time and space to take it all) we found that they had picked through the items and left the boxes (and many, if not most, of the items) sitting there, on the ground. I guess that was the final F-you to us. Did they expect us to load everything back in our car and take it back home? Um, no. That was their stuff. It really wasn't our responsibility to separate it out for them in the first place. It certainly wasn't our responsibility to dispose of it. In fact, we had no authority to touch anything that we had turned over to their attorney. We took a picture of everything, sent that to our attorney and left it all behind.

Fourteen

Repercussions

I awoke the next morning with the worst migraine I had had in months and given that I had been having migraine headaches virtually every day since this whole thing started that was saying something. Somehow, I hoped, this was all the stress and anxiety just trying to work its way out. I cried a lot that day, remembering how awful it had been. But I also cried because of the wonderful support we had received in the week before we went—nearly 50 people were kind enough to email us saying they would be happy to speak on our behalf at either the mediation or a trial, if necessary. The morning of the mediation, I left a cryptic message on Facebook and a bunch of people responded with personal notes expressing their love and support. All of that meant the world to me. It meant we weren't alone in this—there were people out there, even if they didn't know what was going on, who cared and would be there in our time of need. A word here about Facebook and other social media: I'm not a big social media user—I really only have people on my Facebook who I *actually* know. I won't accept a 'friend' request unless I have met you in person and know you, either through work or some other social interaction. I do have a fan page where you can catch up on all the things I'm doing. I guess I'm old-school that way—I like actually getting together with people IRL.

So, our next step was to move. To pack all our stuff and leave our lovely home of the last 18 years and find a new place to live. A new adventure, if you will, since we haven't actually looked for a place to live since… well… the last place we lived before this home and we lived there for probably 10-12 years. So when you add it all together, it's been about 30 years since we've actually looked for a place to live. It's a much different landscape now—you rarely meet the owner of a place. Most places are 'managed' by rental companies and a lot of this stuff is done on-line. It was amusing, to say the least.

One of the 'stipulations' of our settlement was that we would be out—a hard out—by November 1 at 2:00 p.m. The mediation was on July 24th, so that really only gave us three months to find a place, pack up and move. [Just a note: we were actually totally gone by November 1, at 2:00 p.m. but there was nobody there to check and see that we were no longer living at the house. Interesting.] We figured the best plan of action would be to set a deadline for ourselves of October 1. I guess most people don't have deadlines, though, since there seemed to be a general malaise about renting. People took their time getting back to us to show us their place. Or they wanted to 'collect a bunch of applications' and run the credit checks at the same time, meaning we would have to wait a week or two to even hear whether they would rent to us—just delay after delay.

We started packing right away. We started seriously looking over the Labor Day weekend and when it got to be *after* the 20th of September and we still didn't have a firm place yet, we were getting a little antsy. However, one of the first places we looked at was a cute 2-bedroom place just around the corner from where we had lived right before moving up the hill with my Mom and, on a whim, we went back and it was still available. We hadn't acted on it, initially, thinking it was a bit small for the price (and by this time we had seen a couple of 3 bedroom places and 2 bedroom w/den) but so far none of the bigger places were willing to commit and this one had dropped their price. It was now the 25th of September and we needed to make a decision. Our 'fallback' place, around the corner from this one, was doing some construction and the layout of the 2-bedroom apartments wasn't great—it was small and cramped and I couldn't imagine living there for a year. So we came back to this place, put in our application and two hours later the place was ours. Time to buckle down and get to work.

What a comedy of errors trying to fit furniture from a

3300 square foot home into a 1300 square foot apartment. But we did it, with a little help from a couple of storage units. And did I mention that we had already put a bunch of stuff into a storage POD back before my brothers had filed their lawsuit. So this was storage upon storage. Ugh!

Dealing with my 7' grand piano turned out to be a little bit more problematic. There was room for it in the apartment, but getting it either IN the elevator (it didn't fit) or UP two flights of stairs (very expensive) ended up being a deal breaker and we had to put it in storage for the year. Very, very sad. What was I to do when I got an assignment to accompany a choir, soloist or instrumentalist with music that I'd never before seen? I used to just sit down at my piano and familiarize myself with the music so I could play it for them. I'm a pretty good sight-reader, but I'm not *really* comfortable having my first time seeing the music actually BE the performance of it in front of an audience—a sticky wicket indeed. However, just when I thought it was going to be untenable (meaning, I was starting to be asked to play for multiple holiday programs… choirs, soloists, etc.) an angel came out of the woodwork and offered me his electronic keyboard for as long as I needed. It was nothing fancy, but it did give me a keyboard to practice on so I could at least play through the music a few times before it was time to perform. I have the best friends and, as another friend pointed out—things are always working out for me. For that I am truly grateful.

We had my car towed into the shop and fixed so I could start to drive it again, which was no easy (or inexpensive) feat since it had been parked in the garage and not driven for 10 years.

As I was writing this it was mid-2019. Two Christmases had come and gone. The first one we hardly celebrated. It just didn't feel right without my Mom here. We drove up to Sacramento to gift my grandmother's keepsake china to a distant cousin who lives there and then went down to San Francisco and the Bay Area to see if we could recreate some of the feelings we had when we used to visit (when my Mom was still alive). We thought we'd visit Mary Jones again but found that she had passed a few weeks before we got there. We couldn't even bring ourselves to get a tree that year. We drove back to LA on Christmas Day, hoping to avoid traffic. We really weren't in any kind of holiday spirit at all.

By the time the Holidays rolled around this last year we were in a more permanent place, with all our decorations, tree and trimmings to give us a sense of 'home'. It's just unsettling feeling so uprooted, but I guess that's life. And now, as we approach the Holiday season in the midst of a Pandemic… well, life has surely been a roller-coaster of late! LOL!

The lawsuit is over. The house is sold. It's amazing who comes out of the woodwork when there's actual money to be had. The old Trustee decided he was owed money, even though he didn't defend the Trust nor did he attend the mediation. He threatened to sue and when his own attorney gave him the boot (after my attorney told him 'the facts of life') he took his case to Small Claims Court. Eh, I just can't be worried about this stuff anymore. I have to turn my attention to the rest of my life. I've dealt with this stress for too long and I'm just done with it. Life begins again… as it always does.

I don't really feel my Mom around much anymore, although every now and then I hear her whisper some small piece of advice when I need it most. I suppose she's turned her attention to the next adventure. That's as it should be, as well. She deserves to be happy and free and move onto whatever comes next for her. I'm sure it's awesome! I can hear her saying "This is your life, Kathi, I trust you to make the most of it... after all, I taught you to be independent and not to need me."

I remember when I was a kid and I walked myself, alone, to school or to my Sunday School class and I saw the other kids walking with their mothers. I asked her once, "Why don't you walk with me to class?" and she said, "You're a big girl – you don't need me to walk you to class. Besides, my job isn't to baby you, my job, as your mother, is to raise you to be independent of me – not to need me." I guess she did her job, although I kinda wish she was still here because even if I don't *need* her... I sure do *miss* her.

Fifteen

Epilogue

Okay, so I no longer have my brothers in my life and that's hard. Devastating, in fact. I have also been warned that now that the focus of the lawsuit is, for all intents and purposes, over I will truly start to mourn the loss of my mother—something that took a backseat during the stress of everything I have been dealing with.

I have spent quite a bit of time thinking about and working on forgiveness. I have written pages and pages in my journal on it. One of the most transformative exercises I have done was to journal on Accepting the Apology that will Never Come. Ooh. If you've never done that little exercise, let me tell you it's not little by any stretch. It took days and lots of tears. Powerful stuff.

Recently I heard Oprah say that a profound moment for her was when she heard this: "Forgiveness is giving up the hope that the past could have been any different." She went on to say: "It's being able to let go and not being held hostage for another minute by the past."

Part of writing this book has been a letting go. An acceptance of what was done and a release of being held by it. Forgiveness doesn't mean condoning a behavior or turning a wrong into a right. It simply means that you give yourself permission to accept and release that what was done has been done. I no longer want to hold this grudge because I don't want it to hold me. This is my way of releasing it and moving forward with my life. For any of you who are reading this book and holding onto anger, holding onto a grudge, holding onto a wish that the past could be different somehow, my wish for you is to let go. Accept what was and move on. Free yourself from the shackles of "what could have been" and "what should have been" and step into is and what could be.

I know when she was alive my mother would *not* have wanted for me that my brothers end up hating me and abandoning me over money. I also know that coming through this, surviving it intact, stronger in my relationship with my husband, stronger in my sense of self, better able to handle whatever life throws at me and moving forward with peace—that *is* the legacy that she would want for me. And, as I type these words, I can hear her whisper in my heart, "You're right. I always knew you had it in you."

Thanks, Mom. The experience of caring for you is one I will always treasure. It taught me so many things. It is definitely not for the feint of heart, but if one can do it, even for a little while, it will teach you many things and bring much joy. For me, probably the biggest thing I will take away at *this* moment in my life is the fact that it gave me the chance to get to know my mother as a woman—not just as my mother but as a fellow traveler in this thing called life. I really got to 'see' her, all her hopes and dreams, all her faults and failings, her past and present, her fears and strengths. She became real, to me.

KATHI CAREY

Sixteen

Final Thoughts

I put the book away for quite a while, thinking I was finished. However, I started receiving inquiries. People reached out for advice about how to handle caring for an elderly parent, a loved one, someone in the final stages of their life. It occurred to me that, even though I am no expert on the subject, I could impart what little wisdom I had gained from my own experience in the hope that it can help you.

Be aware that these are my own personal experiences and your life and loved ones may be completely different. I'm just sharing what worked for my husband and me with my mother, and, of course, those things we learned along the way. I am also going to share some cautionary advice learned from the trenches of the lawsuit we had to undergo. Hopefully you will never have to endure anything like we did.

Sundowners:

My Mom got sundowners syndrome in the last couple years of her life. As her physical body wore down the symptoms of the sundowners got worse. If you don't know what this is, it's a particular form of dementia that comes on late in the day—as the sun goes down—which is why it is given this specific name. My Mom would get very anxious, scared in fact, not knowing who she was, who we were, where she was or anything. She knew she *should* know these things, which was what scared her. What worked for us was to either tell her things about her early life, when she was young (a child) and recount some of her memorable life experiences or to actually read her life story to her. We were lucky. She had written her life history before she came to live with us and, as we had been going through her things, we found it. So, we would sit and read her life story to her and it 'brought her back.' Often my husband, when reading, would purposefully read something 'wrong.' She would, inevitably, catch him in the mistake. "Really, Mom?" he'd say. "Oh, yes," she'd reply. "That didn't happen like that." "Well, then, how did it happen?" he'd ask. She'd go on to recount exactly how it *did* happen, showing that she was, in fact, recovering her memories, which we could then use as a way to comfort her and appease her fears. Be aware, however, that this will all take a lot of time—hours and hours. Obviously this is service that you're providing to a loved one, so the time required is of no import. But remember this when your house goes uncleaned, the dishes aren't washed, the clothes sit in the washing machine, etc. and don't beat yourself up over it. These are moments you can never recapture. These are the times you will remember when that loved one is gone.

Additional Help:

There is no shame in getting help, if you can afford it. Letting someone else take on some of the chores of caring for your loved one—the cleaning, the changing, the feeding, etc.—can free you up to spend quality time with them. Also, even if you have help, there is no shame in getting respite care, if it is provided for you. Many times hospice will provide for a weekend or a few days of what is called 'respite care' where your loved one can stay in a nursing home while you get a break. Everyone needs a break. Even you. We took a weekend of respite care in order to attend my uncle's funeral. Unfortunately for us, it ended up costing us money, as my mother was no longer able to feed herself and none of the care facilities would take on that additional burden. So, we were forced to hire (and pay) our caregiver to stay with her and feed her for the time that my Mom was in respite care. However, it did give us a break and it was worth it.

Minor Health Concerns:

Some of the things that aren't immediately obvious to you when a loved one is heading toward death are things like: they begin to have a hard time swallowing. Yes. Their normal bodily functions start to fail. For my Mom this happened during the last couple of years. Whenever we tried to give her something to drink (water, juice, etc.) she would start choking on it as her normal swallowing response wasn't working. We had to 'thicken' the fluid with something called… Thicken. This isn't necessarily life threatening (although I suppose it actually could be) and no doctor or nurse ever told us about this—we just had to figure it out ourselves.

Another thing we had to figure out: her teeth. The first thing that happened was she had a toothache. A bad one. Okay. We took her to the dentist and, as it turned out, she had a broken tooth that probably should've been extracted. However, by this time and this age her teeth were starting to calcify, meaning they were becoming part of her bones. What that meant was that her root was deep and in order to get the tooth out a specialist would have had to break the jawbone. Um, no. Too much trauma for a woman her age. We got some ambesol for the pain, which eventually subsided on its own. The second thing we noticed was that she started 'pocketing' her food—meaning she would chew and chew and then put the chewed up food in her cheek until she thought we weren't looking and then spit it out. Time to start mashing up her food into the consistency of baby food. That way she could actually consume it and get the benefits from it, like the vitamins, minerals and protein she really needed, because at this point her teeth weren't actually able to chew much of it anymore.

Bedsores were a concern, although she didn't get one until right before she died. I would chalk that up to a very concerted effort to keep her moving around. If at all possible, its best to move the patient—either sit them up and then actually get them up on their feet—or move their position around in the bed enough so that they aren't in the same position hour after hour. I understand that this can be, literally, impossible. However, once that person gets a bed sore it is almost impossible to heal. As my Mom's skin got thinner and thinner we used patches of a special bandage/skin replacement to, more or less, shore up the thinnest points. This requires a keen eye to notice where the soft spots may be developing. As weak as she got, we were still able to get my Mom on her feet 5 days before she passed. Now, these weren't for long stretches and she didn't walk far, but even a few steps can make the difference between developing a bad bed sore and one that is just on the edge of starting but doesn't actually develop.

Morphine. I'm not sure how I feel about this. I understand why it's used—to alleviate pain. I also understand that when someone is dying it is, most likely, painful. Maybe *really* painful (note: I haven't done it yet, so obviously I can't speak from experience). But I also know that as soon as they upped my Mom's dosage of morphine to more than a couple of drops under the tongue she was gone and she never really came back. Her legs and arms were useless, she was unconscious and it was almost as if she was dead already. This is when she had to be turned, regularly, by the caretaker and hospice nurse, so her bedsores didn't get worse. So, I believe there is a point where morphine needs to be administered so that the patient isn't in too much pain. But I don't think it should be administered to make the caretaker's job easier. My opinion. Yours may vary. This is also when they started giving her Ativan for anxiety. Again, not sure how I really felt about that, but the hospice nurses were absolutely sure that she would feel anxious about dying, so the doses were given. The combo of the two is a real one-two punch of putting someone OUT, which is probably the general idea.

Paperwork:

Ahh, the fun and not-so-fun stuff (I am being a bit facetious here). Let's talk about all the impersonal, but really necessary stuff that needs to be done before someone dies.

Power of Attorney. Yes, you need one. Both a Durable Power of Attorney for all the general stuff and one for Health Care. Someone needs to hold these so that decisions can be made with regard to financial matters, health care matters, and other important things that may happen while the individual is still alive. One of the things that I used my POA for was to draw down monies from my mother's money market account after she was unable to do so herself. These monies were used to pay her health care attendants. She had, originally, been taking care of the draws herself—when she first broke her hip she was still quite able to make phone calls and deal with the agent over the phone. However, as she got weaker and her dementia became more pronounced, it was clear that I needed to take over. It was at that point that they required that I have a POA in order to draw money from *her* account, even though I was her daughter. Thankfully we had taken care of getting that POA when she was still fully functional.

I also used that POA to add myself to her bank account. I had not realized that once she died the POA became, for all intents and purposes, useless. I was given this little tip by my sister-in-law, who had been on *her* mother's bank accounts before *she* died, and was able to pay some of the final bills from that account. So, I used the POA to add myself to my mother's account just days before she passed and, indeed, was able to pay one of her final medical bills from that account after she passed. If you're *not* already on a joint account with the family member who's care you're in charge of, you should make sure you're added to that account, either by that person or by way of a POA so that you can handle the final bills that will be presented after their death.

If your charge doesn't have an "End of Life" statement of wishes, they must have one. They also need to prepare a Durable Power of Attorney for Health Care and appoint someone as their POA in the event that they cannot make health care decisions for themselves. If that's you, then you should understand what their wishes are. I never had this conversation with my mother until a little before she was in hospice. Was she totally 'with it' and did she really understand what I was asking her? Yes, I think so. I made sure to catch her at a time when she seemed to be fully functioning, cognitively, so that she *would* understand. I had tried unsuccessfully to have this conversation some time earlier with my brothers, together and separately, and they each abdicated the responsibility to me. Not great. I felt like they were putting my mother's life in my hands and saying, "We don't want to be responsible—you do it." So be it. It had to be done. So, I picked a time and spoke with her as gently but dispassionately as I could. At that point in time she asked for no heroic measures, but she did want to be revived if it was felt that she could continue living the life that she was currently living. However, a few months later, after her health deteriorated further and she was put into hospice, it was decided that even those measures would not be taken. Obviously, once someone goes into hospice it is understood that there will no longer be any 'heroic measures' taken to keep them alive. It is understood that this is the end, or the ramp up to the end.

One of the most important things that should be discussed with someone before death is where all the important papers and policies are located and how to retrieve them. My mother had told me where these items were when she first moved in with us so I already knew where to find them. She didn't have a lot. But if your person has many things, like a will, a trust, insurance policies, safe deposit boxes and bank accounts, you will need access to all of those or the knowledge of where to find them *before* they pass. You don't want to be looking for this stuff after the fact.

Celebration of Life (or Funeral Arrangements): If you are caring for someone who knows their death is imminent I think it would be a kindness to ask them how they would like their life to be celebrated. Perhaps even to have that celebration before they go. I think one of the saddest things is the fact that we say such wonderful and nice things about people *after they go*. Wouldn't it be better to express all those things to the ones we love *before* they go – while they're still here and can hear and appreciate our loving thoughts and feelings? Obviously that's not always possible and it wasn't with my Mom, although my husband and I spent every day telling her how much we loved her—not a day went by that we didn't tell her, multiple times, that we loved her and were so happy she was living with us. I was also so grateful to be able to express to her all the wonderful things she had accomplished in her life right before she passed. I wanted her to leave with absolutely no regrets—to know that she had done everything she had ever wanted to do in the course of her life. But if you have the chance to sit with your loved one and plan out their final ceremony, or even to have that program while they are still here, how wonderful that would be. At the very least if you know what they want (music, eulogy, life sketch, more informal where people recount memories), then they can have an end of life ceremony that would celebrate *their* life.

Living Arrangements: If one of the things you are planning to do is to live with an elderly parent in order to look after them or take care of them in their last years, like we did, I would suggest that you memorialize your arrangement. Put whatever your agreed-upon arrangement is in writing. Sign, date and have a notary notarize it. If you can't notarize it, at least sign and date it and have someone who isn't a family member witness it. We didn't do this because we all understood that Mom would come to live with us, she'd buy the house and we'd pay all her (and our) expenses in lieu of rent. At least we *thought* we all understood (and by their actions my brothers signaled that they understood since they 'let' us pay for everything having to do with my mother and her care once she moved in with us). However, when Mom decided to leave the majority of the equity in the house to me and my brothers got upset over that and sued me one of the first things they accused me (and my husband) of is that we 'lived off of my mother' and 'lived in the house for free' all those years. All of which was patently false—my mother lived on a fixed income (all she had was social security) and the expenses of the house far exceeded her meager monthly check, not to mention that my brother was borrowing (from her) what amounted to an average of $1,000 per month for the first 10 years we lived together. However, we didn't have anything in writing so how could we go back and reconstruct those conversations that they claim never happened or they didn't remember after her death? Impossible. Put everything in writing. Even with family. You'll thank me later.

Trusts, Wills and Other Bequests: The next thing was when my Mom changed her trust. I believe that she wanted to be fair so at the same time she cashed out one of her IRAs or Money Market Accounts and distributed it to my brothers and not me, telling them it was an 'early inheritance'. She told me that was doing this since she was giving me a bigger share of the house. She indicated she would tell them the same thing. So, in 2006 they each got a nice five-figure check and I got nothing. Cut to 2016 and 2017 and the lawsuit: they "don't remember" any conversation with her to the fact that this was an 'early inheritance' or anything of the sort. In fact, until I provided actual proof, in the form of cancelled checks that each of them received and cashed (that my mother happened to keep) they claimed to have never received *any* money. Once proof was proffered, they claimed the money was a 'gift,' although I'll warrant that neither of them claimed it as such on their taxes and neither did she. And, of course, it would've been totally against my mother's nature to give each of them a 5-figure 'gift' and not give the same to me. Again, if your loved one wants to make any kind of 'gifts' or distributions before their death, whether as 'early inheritance' or to offset some sort of distribution offered in a will or trust, everything should be in writing, notarized and dated so that there is no way people can wriggle out of it at a later date, when the loved one is gone and cannot speak as to their intent. Especially when things can get contentious. Best to have everything spelled out, in black and white, with the help of an attorney who is well versed in these things, so that there's no wiggle room for bitterness or hurt feelings later on.

Look, I understand completely the position that my brothers hold: that their early inheritance in the five figures didn't compare with the way real estate prices had risen in Southern California during the 16+ years we and my mother lived in, and improved, that house. I'm sure they felt (and feel) that they were getting the short end of the stick and that I had somehow cheated them out of their inheritance, regardless of the cash payout each had received. But here's the thing: my mother had no way of knowing that her investment in that home would pay off in such a big way. In fact, during the downturn in 2008 the value of the home went down, like everything else in Southern California. It was her intention to provide a home for my husband and me for the future in exchange for us taking care of her. She fully expected us to continue to live there and buy out my brothers' interest, which we would have done had her wishes (with regard to the Trust) been carried out. So, it really didn't matter whether or not the value of the home had risen substantially – we had no intention of "cashing in" on that as we intended to make that our permanent home.

Paying for Things: My Mom paid into a long-term care policy for many, many years and we were hopeful that it would cover many of the costs that we needed to cover for her at-home care. Unfortunately, she took out a policy that *only* covered nursing home care and it only kicked in after the first 100 days. One hundred days of nursing home care can be quite pricey, depending on where you live and what type of care you're looking at. By the time we were ready to activate the account she most definitely did NOT want to go to a nursing home. In fact, we felt that it would shorten her life – we had seen how her quality of life diminished greatly when she went into the nursing home for just one weekend when we activated the respite care. However, she did have some money that we were able to use for her end-of-life care so we were in luck in that regard, even though it ended up not being enough.

If your parent or loved one has investment or savings accounts set aside to pay for their retirement or for their final years, however those final years will be spent, and those funds are readily available to pay for elder care, nursing home care, etc., lucky you! However, it may well be the case that your person does *not* have money or any type of long-term care policy. Don't be afraid to investigate what State and Federal programs are available to pay the health care costs that are above and beyond MediCare. They can be a life- and money-saver.

Finally, if there is an account or policy that has been put aside to pay for funeral expenses, that should also be in writing somewhere, signed, dated and notarized by the loved one. For as long as I can remember my mother said she wanted her life insurance policy to pay for her funeral expenses – that was what she intended it to be used for. It was purchased way back before she was married in the 1940s so it wasn't much and wouldn't really cover funeral expenses in 2016, but it could have covered *some* of those expenses. However, when I found the policy and called the company they wouldn't speak to me because she had listed my older brother on the policy as the primary beneficiary. By this time we were in litigation so I passed his attorney's information along to them and I was given to understand that he was sent a check from the insurance company and it was cashed. However, it was my *younger* brother who paid for the funeral expenses and had that check gone to the estate there would have been no question that it would have gone to him. Again, something in writing (either in the form of a will or with the insurance company) would have made sure that happened.

Let me make this clear: I am now doing all this for myself. I am writing up my own will, my own eulogy, my own wishes for what is to be done with each of the things that are precious to me. If there is something that means anything to you and you want it to be handled or distributed in a certain way upon your death you should do likewise. As 'they' say, we never know how long we are given in this life. It is best to have our affairs in order, no matter what our age.

Ultimately, when you leave this life you can't take it with you. That's the definitive truth. With that in mind, and seeing just how much my mother collected during her life that my husband and I have been and are still dealing with, I am bound and determined that I am not going to leave a hoarder's paradise behind. I don't have children nor, at this point in time, do I really have any family that cares about any of the 'things' that I own or possess. So, my goal, really, is to let go of the bulk of my possessions – let them go to people who will use them, love them and care for them as I have.

It has been a journey, this book. In some ways writing this has kept my mother's memory vibrant and alive. I almost don't want to be done with it. With that in mind, I have taken to writing a blog. If you have found this book (and my mother) interesting at all you might check it out. I'm posting the letters that my father wrote to my mother during their courtship back in 1946 and 1947. Letter-writing has become a lost art in these days of instant communication by way of email and text but I think reading them, not just my Dad's letters, but any letters from that time period is like visiting a tiny bit of history and catching a glimpse into what people were like a little over 70 years ago. It's funny—nobody, not my friends or my teachers or anyone who ever met my Dad, would call him romantic. Most everyone was a little intimidated by him. He was big and tall (6'3", 250 lbs), fought in WW2, had two Purple Hearts, was whip smart and quite imposing. He liked to tell a WW2 story about when they were behind enemy lines and were supposed to carry their weapons everywhere, even to mess (meals). But there was one day my Dad didn't have his. He was 'dressed down' by a senior officer who was new to the field of conflict and my Dad looked him straight in the eye and said, "Sir, when I got big enough to kill a man with my bare hands, I stopped carrying a weapon." He said the guy blanched, said nothing and never bothered him again. He told the story with a laugh (I think he was secretly messing with him), but he said the guy got the message. These letters show a different side—mushy, romantic, goofy almost. The series is called "My Dear Teddy" on Medium.

KATHI CAREY

About the Author

Kathi grew up with her two brothers and an adopted brother in the shadow of Stanford University where both of her parents attended school. By all accounts she was "gifted" in music and started performing piano in local recitals and concerts when she was about 6 or 7. However, Kathi did not pursue music as a career, opting instead to move to Los Angeles and pursue a career in the film and television business.

Kathi has been living in the Los Angeles area most of her adult life. She initially pursued a career as an actress and found some success there. She also worked as a singer in the showrooms of Vegas, Tahoe and Reno and it was while involved in those endeavors that she met her husband. They formed a duo and sang together for a time, but things changed at the casinos so they returned to Los Angeles and Kathi's focus slowly changed from acting to writing, producing and directing. She has been an award-winning writer, producer and director for a couple decades now and enjoys that work immensely. She still acts occasionally when asked by a colleague, as well as in her own projects.

You can find and connect with Kathi online here:

Twitter: @kathicarey
Instagram: @kathithefilmmaker
Facebook: TheRealKathiCarey
IMDb: imdb.me/kathicarey

www.ingramcontent.com/pod-product-compliance
Lightning Source LLC
LaVergne TN
LVHW051605070426
835507LV00021B/2786